# AFTER
# a DEATH

# AFTER A DEATH

## *Practical Problems – Sensible Solutions*

### SHELAGH CLAYTON

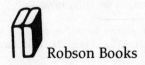

Robson Books

Whilst the advice and factual information contained in this book is believed to be true and accurate at the time of publication and is presented in good faith, neither the author nor the publisher can accept any legal responsibility or liability for any errors or omissions made. Information relating to the law is given solely to enable the reader to understand the legal situation. It is not intended to be, or be a substitute for, professional legal advice. All financial information is subject to change from time to time and the reader is strongly advised to check the situation before taking any action.

Grateful thanks are offered to all those who gave freely of their time and information in the preparation of this book. Particular thanks are given to Mary Fitzgerald for her constant support, Ben James and Amanda White, without whom it would not have happened, for professional legal input from Mishcon de Reya on the subject of Wills and for the assistance of Alan Rice of Tapper Funeral Service, Bournemouth.

First published in Great Britain in 1996 by Robson Books Ltd, Bolsover House, 5–6 Clipstone Street, London W1P 8LE

Book design by Harold King

**British Library Cataloguing in Publication Data**
A catalogue record for this title is available from the British Library

ISBN 0 86051 956 2

Typeset by The Harrington Consultancy
Printed and bound in Great Britain by WBC Book Manufacturers Ltd., Bridgend, Mid-Glamorgan

# Contents

# PART IV – Special Circumstances

# Appendices

# Preface

A death in the family is a devastating experience. In an ideal world the bereaved should have time to grieve and remember. They should be freed from the stress of everyday life to mourn in privacy and dignity. Unfortunately, in our society this is impossible. The bereaved will discover, when they are at their lowest ebb, that burying their dead can be an impersonal and bureaucratic procedure, which turns a deeply loved deceased into 'the body' and grieving relatives into reluctant administrators.

Someone in the family will have to organize the funeral and deal with the estate – the distribution of money or property belonging to the deceased. Instructions about this are usually, but not always, given in a will. The bereaved may well inherit money or mementoes; they will certainly inherit problems. They will find that someone must disentangle the legal and personal commitments that we all undertake throughout our lives – a task often underestimated in its difficulty and complexity.

Typical problems such as finding a new home for a much-loved pet, deciding whether to throw out old love letters or locating a missing insurance policy are time-consuming and distressing, more so because this usually means going through personal files and papers and often seems like an invasion of privacy. Many of these problems have easy solutions, but they are only easy when you know what they are. Other people have faced problems such as these and found the answers. Why re-invent the wheel, especially at time when you need less stress, not more?

This book is based on personal experience and the realization that to bury the dead and succeed in disentangling their private affairs one needs the administrative skills of a bureaucrat, the financial understanding of an accountant and, often, the patience of a saint.

The aim of the book, therefore, is to lead the bereaved step by step through every problem they are likely to face, and to suggest practical ways of dealing with them. Each chapter deals with a specific aspect of bereavement and the problems that arise in the subsequent days, weeks and months, reduces these problems to a series of manageable tasks, and shows how to tackle them. Most importantly, it offers guidance on how to make contact with the many people and organizations that can be relied upon to offer advice and assistance in this difficult period.

NOTE Throughout the text, all references to the deceased, to professional persons, public officials and the like are to 'he', 'him', 'his' – the masculine form. This is simply for the sake of convenience, to avoid having to repeat 'he/she' or 'his/her' each time, which would make the text harder to read. The reader should assume that the text refers to a woman where appropriate. No sexist references are intended by this approach.

The symbols used in this book are:

Ⓗ denoting helpful hints which may be of practical use to the bereaved; and

Ⓣ denoting tasks to be undertaken.

# Part I

# *The Death*

# 1

# How, When and Where

Death, even if expected, is always shocking, no matter how, when and where it occurs. The old cliché is true – death is final. That person will never speak again, or watch TV, or feed the budgie. Their personality has ceased to exist. But their body remains intact, at least for a short time. What do you do with it? Of course, at some stage in the near future the body will be buried or cremated, but what happens to it before then, in the hours immediately after a death? More importantly, if you are present at the death, what should you do and whom should you tell? The answer is, it depends on where the death occurred and why.

## At Home

This is possibly the most distressing scenario, because responsibility for the next steps falls exclusively on the shoulders of those present. Regrettably, these are often family or friends.

### When the death was unexpected

The sudden death of a family member or close friend can leave those present literally stunned and unable to function. What you do is very simple: you call a doctor. There are three reasons for this:

- The doctor will obviously need to confirm that the person is, indeed, dead. If there is the slightest doubt about this, don't wait for the doctor but call an ambulance immediately.

- You yourself, and other family members, may need the reassurance a doctor can provide, and perhaps medication to help you cope with the shock.

- If possible, the cause of death must be identified and a form filled in. The doctor who comes might not always be able to do this, for reasons that will be explained in Chapter 3, but if he can it will save you time and bother later.

1

The doctor you call should, where possible, be the deceased's GP. There are, however, circumstances in which you may not be able to contact him:

- The deceased is not registered with a local GP, or if he is, you don't know which one.

In this case, call for an ambulance – the body must be seen by a doctor.

- Your call to the GP might be transferred to a locum service.

Many medical practices operate an out-of-hours rota whereby one doctor is always on call. Increasingly, however, and especially in towns and cities, they will not do this. Instead, they make use of a service which provides doctors to deal with emergencies. These doctors will not be attached to the GP's practice and will not know you or the deceased personally. They will, however, be fully trained and qualified. Typically, such a service will be run by a controller, and this is the person to whom you will be put through.

When you speak to the controller, explain exactly what has happened and he will arrange for one of the doctors employed by the service to call. Although he will try to attend as soon as possible, be aware that demands on these doctors are often considerable and some time may elapse before he actually arrives. This doesn't mean the death of the deceased is considered unimportant, simply that he may be called out to an emergency somewhere else – to somebody whose life might yet be saved.

## When the death was expected

The situation here is slightly different. If the death occurs during the day, contact a doctor as described above.

If, however, the death occurs at night, and you are absolutely sure the deceased died of his illness, you can either:

- Call the doctor anyway. This is highly advisable, if only to tell him the death has occurred and put the responsibility for what happens next on to his shoulders.

- Leave notifying the doctor until morning. Factors you may want to consider are:
    - The hour at which the death occurred. If there are only a few hours to go until the beginning of the working day, you may feel it is not worth waking a doctor at that time.
    - If you know the GP uses a locum service and there is likely to be an extended delay, you might want to wait

until you can contact the GP personally.
- The feelings of the family: they may be distressed at the thought of the body remaining in the house any longer than necessary and want the doctor's examination over as soon as possible, in order to arrange the removal of the body to the funeral home first thing in the morning.
- Whether any member of the family is in shock or potentially at medical risk as a result of the trauma of the death.

## In Hospital

In this situation, you are effectively a passive observer, sitting by the bedside at the moment of death or perhaps waiting for news in a side room. There will be decisions for you to make very shortly but, for the moment, the medical staff are in charge. Try to listen to any advice they give you about what to do next, but don't worry if it isn't sinking in. Be kind to yourself and allow a few hours for the news to become real: you can always phone the hospital later and ask them to repeat what you have been told.

## In the Street

If you are unfortunate enough to witness a death in the street, take a common-sense approach. Obviously, the first thing you do is to call an ambulance. Give as much detail as you can; for example, if the deceased was choking, say so. Unless you are medically qualified it is conceivable that the victim is still alive: in these circumstances the ambulance crew will be prepared. If the death was clearly caused by an accident, a mugging, or similar, contact the police as well.

## In Suspicious Circumstances

You *must* call the police straight away, or ask someone else to do so. Explain what has happened and they will call an ambulance. Whatever you do, if you are convinced the victim is dead, don't touch or move anything: you might be destroying vital evidence.

## Previously Undiscovered Death

These days, many people live alone. They may be young people who own or rent their own flat or be senior citizens with few friends or relations. Whatever the reason, people who live alone can die in their own home without anyone immediately realizing what has happened.

You may be alerted to the fact that something is wrong by newspapers or mail piling up on the doorstep or in the hall, or by unopened curtains. You may also be contacted by worried friends who cannot get an answer on the phone or from the doorbell and who want to know if you have seen that person recently.

If you have any reason at all to suspect a tragedy (or a crime), call the police at once and leave things to them. Don't forget that breaking into someone's house without permission is illegal. You might, however, have a key to the house, given to you for an emergency such as this, and decide to enter. If you find a body:

- Call the police and tell them what you have found, as you have no way of knowing the cause of death. They will automatically contact the coroner or his officer to attend the scene.

- If you are sure the person is dead, don't touch anything. Leave the house or flat and prevent anyone else from entering.

- Bodies deteriorate after death. Be prepared for this as the deceased, tragically, may have been there for some time. If what you have seen is unpleasant and you are seriously distressed, call your own doctor: he might feel you need some mild tranquillizers to help you over the next few days, or possibly counselling.

## Suicide

If you discover a body and suspect someone has taken his own life, or are present when somebody else makes the discovery, there are two separate things you must consider:

- Contacting the police; and
- Considering the welfare of anyone present who was close to the deceased.

### Contacting the authorities

Whom you call depends on the circumstances. If it is obviously suicide, call the police, who will liaise with the coroner.

### Considering the welfare of those present

There is one certainty, namely that anyone finding a suicide who knew the person in life is going to be profoundly affected. Even if you knew him only slightly, you are going to ask yourself whether you should have seen this coming and whether you missed any cries for help.

If you were close to, or related to, the deceased, your natural grief at a death will be compounded by feelings that you failed him in some way. If he reached out for help you obviously did not see this, or reacted in the wrong way. If he did not reach out to you for help, why not? Did he feel you'd be so lacking in humanity or understanding as to fail to respond? You will feel sorrow, but you are also likely to feel bewilderment and guilt.

The person likely to suffer most is the person who found the body, especially if the method of suicide was unpleasant, such as a hanging. This person will almost certainly be in a state of shock and could well be in hysterics.

Keep an eye on those involved who are still living, as they are certain to need support at the very least and, quite possibly, medical care. (See also Chapter 21). Offer a glass of water or cup of sweet tea if possible. Stay with the distressed person until help arrives and try to appear calm.

## Stillbirth

Call for a doctor or an ambulance as the mother might well have to go to hospital.

While you are waiting for the ambulance to arrive, be as supportive as possible to the mother: the child may never have drawn breath but her grief will be as deep and as real as if it had.

Do not try to prevent the mother from holding the child. There is nothing unhealthy or abnormal about this and, indeed, it can be a very necessary part of the grieving process.

### Miscarriage

In this situation, as far as the mother is concerned, she has lost a child. Treat the situation as if a death has occurred and do not try to minimalize it by suggesting that it was only a foetus which never drew breath.

The main thing to remember is that as soon as a death occurs, you must notify someone who has the authority to deal with the matter. You always need to call a doctor or an ambulance: you may also need to call the police. Don't worry about calling the wrong doctor or phoning at strange hours – these are people who are accustomed to dealing with death. The last thing they will do is tell a shocked relative or witness that they acted foolishly and did the wrong thing.

## Be Kind to Yourself

If you've witnessed a death, you might be glad to speak to a doctor too. These days, there is a better understanding of shock and trauma. Most doctors understand that when they visit immediately after a death, they need to be as concerned with those alive as with the deceased. This includes you, even if you are the person who has assumed command of the situation.

Now, within only a few hours of the death, you will have to start dealing with the many tasks that will arise over the next few days. It isn't difficult as long as you know what is happening and why. The next chapters lay out exactly what you need to do and what your options are.

# 2

# First Tasks

By now the first horrendous few hours have passed. You have begun to accept the death has actually happened and you are starting to wonder what you must do next.

Unfortunately, although making decisions is possibly the last thing on your mind at the moment, you are going to have to start to do so almost immediately. There is also a certain amount of bureaucracy to cope with. All of this will be covered in detail in the chapters that follow, but for the moment what you need is some idea of the tasks you have to tackle in the coming days. This will enable you to plan your time and to call on friends and family for help where necessary.

The following is an overview of the most important things you are going to need to think about.

## ❶ Cope with the Bureaucracy of Death

Bureaucracy is a term frequently used in this book because unfortunately many of the things you must do involve forms or documents. One of your first tasks is to ensure the death is certified and registered.

Each time a person dies in this country, a doctor has to fill in a form to state that the death has occurred and why. This information must then be given to the Registrar, who will record it. This *must* be done – it is a legal requirement. Chapter 3 will tell you exactly what forms are needed and who is to fill them in.

Don't worry about seeing the Registrar on the day of the death: you have five days in which to do so.

## ❶ Decide Whether the Deceased is to be Buried or Cremated

The deceased may have expressed a wish or opinion about burial or cremation during his lifetime. If not, you may want to contact other relatives to see what their views are.

7

If the decision is made to cremate, you will need to warn the doctor (and coroner, if he is involved) as there are special forms that must be filled in to allow a cremation to go ahead. Burials and cremations are discussed in greater detail in Chapters 4 to 6.

## ❶ Organize the Funeral

Although it is possible for friends and relatives to carry out all the funeral arrangements themselves, most people will want to employ the services of a funeral director. Organizing a funeral involves a number of tasks and decisions, and you will need to leave yourself time to handle these properly. It doesn't matter if, for one reason or another, you are unable to set a date for the funeral: you can still go ahead, find a funeral director and start discussing the arrangements. See Chapter 4 for how to go about arranging a funeral.

Call or write to people who need to be notified immediately. These will obviously include close friends and relations, but you should also contact the deceased's bank(s) and employer. All this is explained in Chapter 10.

## ❶ Find and Read the Will

This is one of the more urgent tasks as it may contain instructions from the deceased about his funeral and the disposal of his body. You also need to know whether the deceased has named anyone in his will to manage his estate (such a person is called an executor). See Chapters 13 to 15.

It is also important to find out whether the deceased has left enough money to pay for his funeral. If he hasn't, don't panic: there are several ways round this problem but it is better not to leave this until the last minute. What to do is explained in Chapter 17.

If there is no will, you have to know this as soon as possible. The law lays down a procedure to be followed in this situation and you will want to attend to this as quickly as you can. Chapter 15 explains what actions you need to take.

## ❶ Don't Worry if the Coroner is Called In

You may find that the doctor who has examined the deceased's body is unable to sign the form and instead decides to refer the death to the coroner. A coroner is a person who carries out further investigations into how and why the death took place. He will become involved, basically, in any case where the cause of death is not absolutely obvious and where the deceased hasn't seen a doctor in the fourteen days before the death. If the coroner is called in, the decision to do so will, in almost all cases, be made very soon after the death has been confirmed by a doctor. You must co-operate with his investigation and answer any questions he may ask. All he is trying to do is establish the exact cause of death to enable the body to be freed for the funeral: he is not trying to be obstructive. More information about coroners is given in Chapter 3.

## ❶ Stay as Calm as You Can

You are going to have to do all these things at some stage over the next few days whether you want to or not. If you really think you can't cope, go to your GP and ask him for a mild tranquillizer to help you over this period.

# 3

# Death and Bureaucracy

In this country no burial or cremation can take place unless the cause of death is known, and such information officially recorded by the state. This certification and registration is a legal requirement, and the thought of having to handle the procedure can be daunting if you are not sure what is involved. Establishing the cause of death is something the doctors will do, but exactly how do you go about registering a death? Are there forms to fill in, and if so, which ones? And what on earth is a coroner? It is bad enough trying to deal with officialdom in normal circumstances, let alone when you are being torn apart by grief and unable to think straight. At the back of your mind is the terrible thought that if you get something wrong the funeral will be delayed. You will have messed up one of the last acts you can perform for the deceased. Don't worry: it's easy.

The good news is that there are simple procedures to follow, and most of the work is done by someone else. In the vast majority of cases you are simply a glorified messenger, carrying news of the death from the doctor to the Registrar. One reason why this can't be done by post is that you will need to provide the Registrar with a few simple pieces of information about the deceased, and you will also need to sign something.

The not-so-good news is that there are two possible scenarios, depending on the circumstances of death. Let's call them Situation One and Situation Two.

**❶ Find Out From the Doctor Whether the cause of Death is Known or Not**

### Situation One. Cause of Death Known

Sometimes the circumstances surrounding the death are so straightforward that the deceased obviously died of natural causes. One example of this is where the deceased had been suffering from a life-threatening illness and this was the clear cause of death. To qualify as a Situation One case, the deceased must have been seen by his doctor within fourteen days of death occurring.

As already explained, you are a glorified messenger, carrying forms the doctor will give you to the Registrar. Don't worry if you don't know who this is: it will be explained on pages 17 to 20.

### What forms will I be given?

You will be given a form known as The Medical Notification of  Cause of Death. This will be provided by the doctor and filled in by him. The information it will contain is:

- The date on which the doctor last saw the patient alive.

- The cause(s) of death.

- A statement as to whether a doctor has seen the deceased since the death occurred.

Filling in this form is often known as 'certifying the death'. Be aware that this form is *not* the Death Certificate.

Attached to this on a removable section is the notice to informants. This tells you who can register the death and what information the Registrar is going to require from you. Exactly what information you need to provide is explained in the section on Registration on page 18.

Normally, these will be handed to you by the doctor or a member  of the nursing staff in a sealed envelope.

### Can any doctor fill in this form?

Any doctor can fill in this form provided that certain conditions are met. A doctor can certify the death if:

- He has no doubt whatsoever about the cause of death; *and*

- He has seen the deceased within fourteen days prior to the death.

Both conditions have to be fulfilled. The doctor might be totally and absolutely convinced of the cause of death, but he still cannot sign that certificate unless he saw the deceased within those fourteen days.

He does, of course, need to have seen the body.

**H**   Don't worry about this. Doctors fill in these certificates often during their working lives and you can trust them to know what to do. This information is simply to let you understand what forms you are being given and why.

**ⓗ**   If the death took place in hospital and you are still unsure about these forms, ask one of the nurses. They know all about them, and often seem more approachable than the doctors.

## What do I do then?

You have to decide whether you are a person entitled to register the death (see page 17). If not, give the forms to someone who is. You (or the person to whom you gave the forms) *must* go in person because the Registrar will need to ask you a few basic questions about the deceased and you will be required to sign something.

## What will I be given?

Sorry – more forms. The important one is a green form which you give to the funeral director (see page 19). Without this, the funeral cannot go ahead.

In brief, you need to:

● Make sure the doctor gives you the medical certificate.

● Check you are a person entitled to register the death by reading pages 17 to 18.

● Make sure you have all the information the Registrar will need.

● Go and register the death.

### Situation Two. Cause of Death Not Yet Known

In all other cases, there has to be an investigation to find out exactly what caused the death. Sometimes, the cause might seem blatantly obvious to you and you wonder why this investigation has to take place. It is because there must be no ambiguities or unanswered questions. Take, for example, the situation where a frail old lady dies in bed in a cold room. It is important to know whether she died of natural causes or whether it was the cold that killed her. If it was natural causes, nothing could have prevented her death. If it was the cold, she might have lived months or even years had the room been heated. The reason for these enquiries starts to become more obvious: if a large number of pensioners are dying from the cold there is clearly a problem, and statistics collected from these investigations might result in government action to help the elderly.

There are other cases where it is more obvious that further questions must be asked. If, for example, the old lady in the example above had bruises round her neck, this might well be an indication of foul play. If the investigations show that there was, indeed, foul play, a criminal investigation can begin.

These questions are asked by the coroner. By law, he has to be called in wherever there is a Situation Two case, that is, where a doctor is unable to sign The Medical Notification of Cause of Death certificate. You can see, therefore, that it is quite common for the coroner to be called in, and you should be prepared for this. The practical effect is that you cannot set a date for the funeral until the coroner has completed his investigations.

Who decides whether it is a Situation Two case? Very simple. It is the state. The law lays down a list of circumstances in which the coroner must be called in. Anyone can call the coroner in, but in practice it is usually the doctor. He has absolutely no choice over the matter: if the circumstances of the death fall within the state's list, he must contact the coroner. Personal feelings and beliefs have nothing to do with it.

## The coroner

The coroner is either a qualified lawyer or a doctor, and occasionally both. As explained above, he must be called in by the doctor when he is unable to sign The Medical notification of Cause of Death certificate. The state is quite clear as to the circumstances in which this must be done, and these are when:

- The deceased had not been seen by a doctor within fourteen days of the death.
- When death was caused by:

  An accident.
  Suicide.
  Abortion.
  Drugs.
  Poison.
  Industrial disease.
  Military service.
  Anaesthetics given during an operation.

- When death took place:

  In policy custody.
  In prison.

- When the general circumstances of the death are suspicious.

As you can see, many deaths are going to fall into one or other of these categories, and this is why in practical terms a coroner will often be called in when a death has occurred. In most cases, this is little more than a formality. However, once a coroner has been called in, the body cannot be released for burial until the coroner has completed his enquiries, so it is in everyone's interest to identify the cause of death as quickly as possible.

## What happens when the coroner has been called in?

When the coroner has been called in, he will question you, the doctor(s) and anyone else he believes might have useful information. In the simplest cases he might only need to speak to the GP and you will know little or nothing about the enquiry. In other cases he will need to speak to several people. It is quite possible that he will do this on the day of the death or soon after, so as not to delay the burial.

The questioning is obviously a distressing experience, especially as it takes place so soon after the death, but most coroners are sympathetic and helpful and try to make the interview as stress-free as possible. You are not going to be asked any sinister questions. The coroner might, for example, ask whether the deceased suffered from dizzy spells or had a history of crossing roads carelessly.

**ⓗ** Don't be tempted to lie to the coroner to try to avoid a post-mortem. Lying to a coroner could get you into trouble and this is the last thing you need at the moment.

All he is trying to do is to build up a more complete picture of what happened in order to get at the truth. As long as there is no suggestion of foul play, the interview will be short and the coroner may not need to see you again. The coroner will also review the medical evidence and if necessary, speak to hospital staff and the deceased's GP. This whole process might well be over in less than a day.

## What does the coroner do then?

The coroner can do one of three things. After speaking to the GP, he can elect to do nothing as, although the GP may not have seen the deceased in the last fourteen days, he is quite sure as to the cause of death. The coroner will issue Form 100 to the Registrar to confirm that he has been notified but will take no further action. Secondly, the coroner can order a post-mortem or, thirdly, a post-mortem and an inquest.

## What is a post-mortem?

A post-mortem is where the body, or part of it, is cut open to enable the doctors to see the exact nature and extent of the injuries or disease and, where necessary, to take samples for analysis. This takes place as soon after the death as possible, often within twenty-four hours. Quite often, this confirms what everybody suspected all along and you can then register the death and set the date for the funeral.

## Can I refuse permission for a post-mortem?

Most people find the thought of a post-mortem offensive for emotional or religious reasons, but the thing to remember is that once the coroner decides a post-mortem is necessary you have almost no choice but to accept this. You are entitled under the law to apply to the High Court to prevent the post-mortem from taking place, but your reasons have to be very strong for this to be granted. The fact that you find it distasteful is not considered sufficient. In the vast majority of cases, you have no choice but to accept the coroner's decision.

**(H)**   Talk with the hospital chaplain or the nurses if you find you cannot come to terms with the thought of a post-mortem.

What you can do, if you wish, is to choose a doctor to be present, although you will have to pay him, and this can be expensive.

This is without doubt the worst stage in the whole process; you feel that the state has taken control and that the deceased has been deprived of all dignity. The truth is the state *has* taken control. The only advice one can give is to try not to think about what is involved. For this reason, and because the coroner knows the body cannot be released until he has reached a decision, the post-mortem is likely to take place quickly, sometimes with startling speed. The only good news is that you are unlikely to have long to dwell on the prospect.

**(H)**   Because the post-mortem usually occurs with very little delay, you will not be forced to agonize about it during weeks of sleepless nights. Concentrate on some other task – there will be enough of them. Phoning around local funeral homes to get comparative quotes of services is a useful task at this stage and will, perhaps, help to divert your attention (topic discussed in Chapter 4).

## Who pays for the post-mortem?

The council. It will cost you absolutely nothing.

## Will I be told the results?

Surprisingly, the coroner has no legal duty to inform the next of kin of the results of the post-mortem. As a rule he will phone you directly or arrange for the news to reach you by some other means. It is worth checking, however, that this will happen. If it does not, you must phone the coroner's office to get the results. The cause of death will be given on the Death Certificate.

## After the post-mortem

Usually, after the post-mortem, the coroner and the medical staff know enough to decide on the cause of death. If this is the case, the coroner will write this information on a certificate, the Pink Form, and in most cases send it to the Registrar (in theory it can be given to you, but this doesn't often happen). You must still go in person to see the Registrar as there is something for you to sign, and he will need to ask you a few questions (see page 17 onwards).

If, however, the coroner feels that there are still unanswered questions, there must be an inquest. This is relatively rare (see Chapter 19). Most people, fortunately, will be able to claim the body of the deceased by this stage and set a date for the funeral.

So, taking a Situation Two case step by step:

- Wait as patiently as you can for the coroner to complete his enquiries.

- When he has done so, check that you are a person entitled to register the death.

- Go to the Registrar (remember – you won't have a form to take) and complete the registration.

## I'm confused. Which forms will I be given?

Situation One: you get a certificate in a sealed envelope (which is a medical certificate and a notice to informants).

Situation Two: you don't get a form at all. The coroner will send it by post. (It is just possible he will give it to you but that is not common).

## ❶ Register the Death

You must, by law, go to the Registrar and register the death within five days of its occurring. This five-day period can be extended to nine days if the Registrar receives written confirmation that the medical certificate has been signed. While you are there, you will be asked for some basic information about the deceased. This information will be recorded in the Register, which you will then have to sign. In return, you will be given some more forms. It is quite possible that this whole process will take less than half an hour.

It might be helpful for you to know a little more about Registrars and registration.

## The Registrar

The Registrar's job is to register all the births, marriages and deaths that occur in one geographical area. A death must be registered in the district in which it occurred. You will find his address in the phone book, at the post office or at the local police station. You don't need to make an appointment – just turn up during opening hours.

ⓗ  If you don't know where the Registrar is to be found, look in the phone book under the name of your local authority or borough. If you still can't find it, phone the police station or go to a Citizen's Advice Bureau. They will be pleased to help.

## Are you entitled to register the death?

The Registrar will check that the deceased lived (or died in hospital) within the area for which he is responsible and that you are a person entitled to register the death.

The state, naturally, provides a list of people who can do this, and further complicates things by making different rules depending on whether the death took place in a building or outdoors.

Don't worry: for all practical purposes most people involved with the deceased can register a death. These people are:

- Where death takes place inside a building: a relative present during the last illness or at the death; a relative who lives within the area administered by the Registrar, or who happens to be in that district. If you are not a relative you can still register the death if: you were present at the death; you are an occupier of the house in which the deceased lived and knew about the death; or you are responsible for making the funeral arrangements.

- Death out in the street: any relative who knows enough about the deceased to answer the questions the Registrar will ask; if you were there at the time of death or found the body; if you are responsible for the funeral arrangements; when the body can't be identified, the police.

The Registrar will ask which of these categories you fall into.

If you don't feel you belong to one of these categories, phone the Registrar and talk it over with him first. One thing you cannot do is delegate this responsibility to someone ineligible, for example, a family friend who has no involvement with the deceased, was not there at the time of death, is not involved in organizing the funeral and who lives in another part of the country. They may offer to help for a few days and take the task off your hands. Sorry – this is illegal.

## What then?

You are now in the Registrar's office and it has been established that you can register the death. If you have been given some forms, hand them to the Registrar.

These forms will be *either* the medical certificate and notice to informants in a sealed envelope *or* (in very rare cases) a Pink Form from the coroner.

The Registrar will then ask you a few questions about the deceased.

## What questions will the Registrar ask?

All he is after is enough information to identify the deceased. He will want to know:

- The deceased's full name.

- If the deceased was a married woman, her maiden name.

- The deceased's usual address (that is, his home address, not an address he was temporarily staying at, such as your home).

- If the deceased was a man, his occupation (or a statement that he was retired, if this was the case).

- If the deceased was a married woman, her husband's name and occupation.

- The deceased's date of birth and place of birth.

- The date and place of the deceased's death.

- Whether the deceased was receiving a pension.

You might well know the answers to all these questions off the top of your head, but it is always worth bringing something like the deceased's passport to this interview in order to make sure the information is absolutely correct. You are asked to bring along the deceased's medical card.

**H** The deceased's passport will contain a lot of this information if you don't know it.

**H** You are requested to take the medical card but don't panic if you can't find it: this is not going to hold up proceedings.

The Registrar will then register these facts.

## How will this be done?

'Registering' means writing these details (using a fountain pen) in a large book, the Register of Deaths. Seeing this done is something of a shock for those who believe that Local Authority records are computerized, but of course there is a sound reason – computer files can be altered and this is information which must not be tampered with.

When the death has been 'registered', the Registrar will ask you to sign the book in which the details have been written. The bad news is that you are about to acquire some more forms.

## Which forms will I be given?

The Registrar will write the information you have just provided (this time often using a computer) on two forms. These forms are:

- The Certificate of Burial or Cremation (known as the Green Form). This form gives you official permission to bury the deceased, or to apply for a cremation to take place. (It is very important to remember to give this to your funeral director.)

- The Certificate of Registration of Death. This is the form you give to the Department of Social Security. It notifies them of the death and starts the process if you need to claim widow's benefit (see Chapter 17). When you get home, fill in the back of this form and send it off in the pre-addressed envelope the Registrar will provide.

You will not have to pay for either of these forms.

## Is either of these the Death Certificate?

No. You need to ask the Registrar for this.

## What is a Death Certificate?

This is a copy of the information written in the Register and is essential when winding up the deceased's estate. You will have to pay for this, unlike the forms you have just been given: the current cost is £2.50. If you can afford it, buy five copies, one for your files and the rest to send out, for example, to an insurance company.

**H**   Make sure you keep these copies in a safe place, as official bodies such as banks, building societies etc. will need to see one. Take a folder with you to put them in.

## Is there anything else the Registrar will give *me*?

There are leaflets that the Registrar can give you, such as information on widows' pension and tax rights, if you ask. He can also issue additional certificates in specialized circumstances. Rather than go into these here, as they will not be required in most cases, ask the Registrar what other help he can give in case you need it.

You have now completed all the tasks in order to register the death of the bereaved in a Situation One or Situation Two case. (For the registration of stillbirths, see Chapter 18.)

### Summary: Who Does What?

The doctor(s)

- Establishes how, when and why the death occurred.

- Gives you medical certificate and notice to informants

or

- Refers the case to the coroner.

The Registrar

- Establishes that the death took place in the area he covers.

- Records the fact of the death and details about the deceased.

- Gives you:
  - Certificate for Burial or Cremation (also known as the Green Form);
  - Certificate of Registration and Death;
  - Death Certificate (if you choose to purchase one).

## Yourself
either

- Ask a doctor to certify the death.

- Tell Registrar about death.

- Take medical certificate to Registrar if not a coroner's case.

- Answer a few questions about the deceased.

- Sign Death Register.

or

- Answer coroner's questions.

- Go to Registrar when his enquiries are complete.

## The coroner

- Reviews evidence to see if death due to non-natural causes.

- Orders post-mortem if appropriate.

- Issues Pink Form if no inquest is to be held.

- Holds inquest if appropriate.

## Certificates

Throughout this chapter mention has been made of various certificates which are issued by different people in different circumstances. This can be confusing and it is worth recapping what certificates you are likely to need and under what circumstances.

### Certificates from the doctor or coroner

| Circumstances | Certificate | Purpose |
|---|---|---|
| Death not referred to coroner | Notice to informants | Tells you about registering the death |
| Death not referred to coroner | Medical certificate | States cause of death and is used for registration |
| Coroner called in but no inquest | Notification by the Coroner (Pink Form) | States cause of death and is used for registration |
| Post-mortem and body to be cremated | Certificate for Cremation (Yellow Form) Rarely seen. | Allows you to apply for cremation, via the funeral director |

## Certificates from the Registrar

| Certificate | Purpose |
| --- | --- |
| Certificate for Burial or Cremation (Green Form) | Gives permission for the body to be buried or application for cremation to be made |
| Certificate of Registration of Death | To notify Social Security. Only fill it in and send it if it applies to the deceased |
| Death Certificate | Legal notice of death – helps you wind up deceased's estate |

In a Situation One case, therefore, the doctor will give you a notice to informants and a medical certificate. When you take these to the Registrar you will receive a Certificate for Burial or Cremation (Green Form), a Certificate of Registration of Death and a Death Certificate. You must give the Green Form to the funeral director.

In a Situation Two case, the only difference is that in most cases the coroner will not give you a form to take to the Registrar, but will send it straight to him. The form he sends to the Registrar is the Notification by the Coroner (Pink Form). The Green Form is only issued if there is to be a burial.

If you want a cremation rather than a burial you have some more form-filling to do, and this is covered in Chapter 6.

Once you understand roughly what is entailed it is best to see the visit to the Registrar as an information exchange involving a number of small tasks. The whole visit will be over in a very short time and then you can concentrate on the funeral arrangements.

# 4

# Arranging a Funeral

## What Is a Funeral?

You are about to spend a considerable sum of money. It is unlikely to be much below £1,000 and may be considerably more. What you purchase will probably last less than two hours. What purpose does a funeral serve, and is it worth the money?

People use the word 'funeral' as if its meaning were the same to everyone. This, of course, is not true. To some, a funeral is a public tribute: to others, it is a highly personal act of love. To some it is a whole process – the viewing of the body, a religious service, the burial or cremation, and perhaps a wake afterwards. To others, it means paying a funeral director to take and bury the body as quickly and with as little fuss or ceremony as possible. This is unimportant. What matters is that the deceased's last journey should be right for him and for those who mourn his passing.

### Do you have to have a funeral?

No, you don't. Legally, all you have to do is to make sure the death is registered correctly and that the body is disposed of.

### What purpose does a funeral serve?

The practical purpose of a funeral, whether organized by a funeral director or carried out solely by the deceased's relatives, is to dispose of the body by burial or cremation.

The main purpose as far as the deceased's friends and relatives are concerned is to allow them a specific occasion on which they can mourn together, unhindered by the pressure of other tasks which have to be carried out. The day of a funeral is a kind of gateway between the past, in which the deceased lived, and the future, in which he will not exist as a person who can be seen and touched. It gives the mourners the chance to remember shared moments of pleasure and ask the deceased's forgiveness for harsh words and neglectful acts. Because everyone knows funerals are emotional occasions, there are no social barriers to showing this grief openly.

23

By saying goodbye in this way, those close to the deceased can start to move forward to acceptance of the death, and the reality of a future without the deceased.

Funerals can also be a public statement that the deceased existed and made an impact on the world. Friends and business colleagues, as well as relatives, can turn up to show that the deceased's life touched theirs at some point, and that they thought sufficient of him, having worked or socialized with him, to make the effort of saying goodbye.

In this sense, therefore, funerals are for the mourners rather than for the deceased. This is something that should be borne in mind when designing the funeral: it is not only what you think the deceased would have wanted for himself, but also what is going to give comfort to those who loved him. This might mean doing something that may mean absolutely nothing to you, or indeed might not have had importance to the deceased, such as ensuring there is a religious service at which the surviving spouse and relatives can pray for the deceased's soul.

Some people might view the whole matter differently. They might feel that the deceased's personality was what mattered, and because that has ceased to exist his body should be interred with the minimum of fuss. Just because they choose to keep the funeral arrangements as minimal as possible does not mean they don't care, simply that they have a different way of expressing it. If this attitude is in line with your own thinking, and that of those close to the deceased, do not feel pressured into making arrangements that mean nothing to you simply as a public display.

## Is it worth the money?

Grief can last for a long time; if you lose someone very close to you, there may be moments for many years to come in which you feel the loss as sharply as you do today. If something can be done to give comfort, however brief, to you or those close to the deceased, and allow you to feel you've said goodbye properly, this surely is worth the expense involved.

How much money you spend is of course up to you, the state of your finances and the amount of money the deceased has left. In the past, people would literally spend their last handful of coins on a funeral in order to give the deceased 'a good send-off'. Today, we realize that the living must be taken care of first: would the deceased really have wanted you to go deep into debt for years to come in order to give him a grandiose funeral?

Whether a funeral is worth the money depends, therefore, on how much you can afford to spend and your emotional needs after the death. It is hard, at that time, to stand back and balance emotional need with a bank statement, but if you do not – if you pay out money you can't afford or which the deceased's estate cannot bear, you are likely to worry about this. The funeral will then turn into one more item to cause you concern and you will not gain from it the full benefit that you otherwise could have done.

Most people choose to buy the services of a funeral director. By doing so, they are purchasing expertise and peace of mind. The funeral director will be able to take many tasks off their hands, and consequently at a time of great stress you are not rushing around trying to order a coffin or worrying that the hearse you hired will have to park on a double yellow line outside the church. This time for saying goodbye should be free of anxiety. Looking back in years to come, you should be able to feel that you did your best. Perhaps it wasn't the most expensive funeral in the world but it went smoothly and the deceased was treated with respect throughout. You will not have to live with the guilt of having organized a botched job as your last service to your friend or loved one.

An increasing minority these days believe, however, that a funeral organized by outsiders is cold, heartless and exactly what they do not want. For those who feel that they, or the deceased, would wish the funeral arrangements to be dealt with exclusively by friends and relatives, the good news is that there are no legal barriers. The fact remains, nevertheless, that organizing a funeral is time-consuming, especially if no thought has been given to the task before the death.

That is not to say that a DIY funeral is undesirable, simply that it takes organization and know-how. If there is any reason to believe that you or your friends or relatives would want such a funeral, it would be sensible to do some research beforehand, so that everyone knows exactly what has to be done when the occasion arises.

The most important thing is that the funeral is appropriate to the deceased, to friends and to relatives, and that there are no major disasters.

## Organizing a Funeral

In Victorian times, sex was a taboo subject but death was openly discussed and extravagantly celebrated. These days, the pendulum has swung completely the other way. An evening in front of the television and a quick flip through some magazines will tell you all you ever wanted to know about sex, and much you did not, but it is virtually impossible to find information on how to bury your dead –

what you must do, what your alternatives are and how much it is all going to cost. It is a subject that is simply not discussed. Whatever the procedure is, it takes place behind the closed doors of a funeral home. All you ever see is the end result – the hole in the ground at the cemetery or the service at the crematorium.

Because of this, when you are faced with organizing a funeral, the number of individual tasks involved can come as something of a shock. You not only have forms to fill in, but you must also liaise with ministers of religion, cemeteries or crematoria, perhaps organize flowers, arrange transport... the list is endless. Although there is no law to prevent the bereaved burying their own dead, the amount of work involved quickly persuades most people to hire the services of a funeral director.

Unfortunately, because of the widespread ignorance of a funeral director's range of skills and responsibilities, you might still be handling tasks that can be taken off your shoulders at a time when you need space to think and grieve. The old image of a funeral director as an ill-educated, dour-faced man in a black suit, who does unspeakable things to the deceased in a basement fitted with tubes and gullies, has been totally overtaken by events. These days, a funeral director is a well-trained organizer, whose main task is to liaise with all the people and organizations concerned, and who sees his job as an essential social service.

But what exactly is involved in organizing a funeral? Which tasks are the responsibility of the funeral director, and which are down to you? Perhaps most important of all, how much freedom do you have to design a funeral that is right for the deceased and for those left behind? The rest of this chapter will take you step-by-step through the arrangements needed for a funeral and will consider the options available to you.

Before looking at the funeral itself, it might be helpful to understand a little about the funeral industry and how it operates, to take away some of the mystique.

## The funeral industry

The funeral industry is neither run, subsidized nor regulated by the state. Each funeral home is a profit-making business which may be independent or may be part of a larger chain. The practical effect of this is that there are no standard fees for funerals: each funeral home is likely to quote slightly different prices and perhaps offer slightly different services.

The funeral industry is self-regulating and many funeral homes are members of a trade association, such as the National Association of Funeral Directors (NAFD) and the more newly formed Funeral Standards Council. These organizations have a code of conduct, which should be made available to you on request or displayed prominently on a wall in the funeral home. Membership of one of the trade associations is also often displayed on their literature and advertisements in, for example, Yellow Pages. If not, don't be shy about asking whether or not the funeral home belongs to a trade association. It is not an absolutely infallible indication of good service but it is a sign that they are are aiming for certain standards, and it will give you redress if you have any complaints at a later stage.

## Funeral directors

This is the proper term for staff in a funeral home who organize funerals. The old term, undertaker, is no longer used as it conjures up a rather crude and old-fashioned image which no longer reflects a funeral director's skills and approach.

These days, a funeral director is a manager who organizes all the different aspects of a funeral, such as removal of the body from the hospital or home, and liaison with the minister of religion.

A funeral director will have had considerable training, both in-house or on one of the many courses that are run nationwide. His training will have covered a number of different areas, such as:

- Knowledge of relevant laws and bureaucracy.
- The funeral needs of people of different faiths.
- General care of the deceased in the funeral home.
- General organizational tasks.
- Support for the bereaved.
- Repatriation of bodies from foreign countries.
- Arrangement for burial abroad.

It is fair to say that nowadays many funeral directors see their job primarily as one of liaison between the various people and organizations involved in a funeral.

## Funeral homes – what are they like?

Funeral homes (which used to be called funeral parlours) are the places from which funeral directors operate. They will typically consist of an entrance area, a separate room in which you can discuss your needs, a chapel of rest where you can view the deceased if you wish, and other rooms in which the embalming and other processes take place. These rooms are almost never accessible to the general public. You can be absolutely sure that there will be no unpleasant sights or smells; indeed, the overwhelming impression is likely to be that someone has been very busy with an expensive tin of furniture polish. Quite often, you will see useful leaflets displayed, and it is always worth collecting these to add to your knowledge of what options you have. It is quite acceptable for you to call in and discuss your needs without making an immediate commitment, and funeral homes are geared to deal with these enquiries.

## Finding a Funeral Home

Someone close to you has died, or is dying. You know you want to employ a funeral director – so exactly how do you start? There are three ways in which you can approach this problem, assuming you haven't had to do this before.

### By recommendation

This clearly is the best way. Ask your friends and relations: if they themselves haven't had to organize a funeral, it is quite possible they are in contact with someone who has. In this way you might be pointed towards a funeral home which is reasonably priced and caring: almost as important, you might hear of ones to avoid.

Most people, however, organize few funerals in their lives, which is why there is such a small pool of knowledge on the subject. It may well be that no one you know has been in this situation.

### Consult a minister of religion

Try your local minister of religion. Unless he is new to the area he will have officiated at many funerals organized by a number of different funeral homes, and he may well be prepared to offer a quiet word as to which to approach and which to avoid, although this advice might well be off the record.

### Yellow Pages

The Yellow Pages are an absolute must for anyone tackling the necessary tasks after a death, and never more so than when you need to find out which funeral homes operate in your area. Scribble down the names, addresses and telephone numbers of three or four funeral homes within easy reach, and give them a ring. Be aware that many funeral homes have an 'out-of-hours' number: you need not wait until the next working day unless you want to.

## ❶ Compare Quotations From Different Funeral Directors

As discussed above, funeral homes are businesses in a competitive market and their prices will vary, sometimes by as much as several hundred pounds for basically the same service. You would be very sensible to contact more than one and obtain quotes, which the funeral home should be able to provide immediately. Don't feel the slightest bit embarrassed about doing this – it is common practice.

Also, do not forget that you don't have to phone – you can always walk in off the street and ask for their prices. This is a good idea if you can spare the time, as you can talk to the funeral director and get a feel for his competence and understanding. If the funeral home cannot cope with your visit, you should wonder whether they are people you wish to deal with. You are about to part with a relatively large sum of money and you want to make sure the funeral home delivers a good service.

Obtaining these quotations also has the advantage that by comparing prices and discussing the matter either in person or on the phone, you can gain a greater appreciation of what is involved, and the different elements you need to consider. This means that when you make a decision it is an informed decision. You are not just saying 'yes' to the first funeral you are offered, simply because you did not realize how much choice is available to you.

One final word on finding a suitable funeral home. Any reputable establishment, whether a member of a trade association or not, will provide in writing a detailed estimate of the services you have requested and the total cost. A funeral home which is not prepared to do this should be treated with the greatest caution. It is wise to ask yourself why they are not prepared to offer one when the vast majority of homes are ready to comply. You may end up with an unpleasant surprise and a bill that is considerably larger than you anticipated or can afford.

❶   It may be obvious, but worth a reminder. Keep all quotations together in one file. If they are left lying loose on a table one could easily be lost or have coffee spilt on it. It is perfectly acceptable to ask a funeral home for a quote once, but you might feel rather awkward doing so a second time.

### What items should be included in an estimate?

You may still be unsure of what kind of funeral you want and how much you can afford to pay. However, you need to know roughly how much it is going to cost and who will offer the best value for money. A sensible approach is to ask for the cost of a basic funeral and find out what exactly this includes. This achieves two things. First, you can make a direct comparison of estimates and get a feel for whether a funeral home's charges are reasonable or extortionate. Second, looking at the package on offer will help you decide whether you want, or can afford to pay more for extra services over and above those offered. If so, you can always phone the funeral home for more information.

Items you should look for in the estimate are provision by the funeral home of:

- Removal of the deceased to the funeral home.
- Coffin (with make specified).
- Hearse/limousine(s).
- Use of Chapel of Rest.
- General care of the deceased.
- Bearers.

This overall package may vary. One funeral home might, for example, include the use of a limousine for mourners where another might charge extra for this service.

One thing you should ask about in particular is embalming (see page 36). Some funeral homes do this as a matter of course: others offer it as an option. If you do not want the process carried out and it is included in the overall price, you will be paying money for a service you don't want.

There are also other expenses which the funeral home will pay on your behalf but which will be charged to you in the overall bill. Typically, these will be fees to the crematorium or cemetery covering use of facilities and, for example, the services of gravediggers and a minister of religion – it comes as something of a surprise to most people to discover that they charge for conducting a funeral, but they do. These charges should be the same no matter which funeral home you approach.

If the deceased is to be buried, be aware that you will also need to pay for a grave, if a plot has not already been arranged. (See Chapter 5).

Thus, by asking around in this way, you can see who offers the best value for money.

It sounds obvious but remember you will get exactly what you ask for, and nothing more. If, for example, the funeral home tells you that for the quoted price they will collect the body in working hours, you can assume that asking them to transport the deceased in the evening or over a weekend will cost extra. Look carefully at the quotes to see what is *not* there and ask whether the service is possible and how much extra it will cost. The same applies to charges by other individuals, such as ministers and organists.

The kind of services for which a funeral home might charge extra are collecting the body from a long distance away, opening the Chapel of Rest during unsocial hours to allow viewing of the deceased, and use of cosmetics on the deceased. You should also expect to pay extra if you want an organist at the church service and special flower arrangements in the church.

### Cost

This, of course, will vary from one funeral home to another, and will also depend on how many of the funeral director's different services you purchase. However, you should be prepared to pay around £1,000 in total for a basic funeral. This will not include the cost of a grave, which can be considerable (see Chapter 5). It is possible to find funerals that cost less, and this by no means necessarily indicates that the standard of service is lower. It might be that the funeral home is situated in a part of the country where costs, generally, are low or perhaps the area has a large number of wealthy people who purchase expensive funerals, enabling the funeral home to reduce the price of a basic funeral. You need to follow your instinct on this, and see whether you think the funeral home is caring and competent.

### What then?

You have obtained your quotes, which you should be able to do within twenty-four hours at the most, and now have a better idea of what a funeral involves and what it costs. Where do you go from here?

### ❶ Make Your Choice and Sign an Agreement

When you have made your choice, you will need to call in and sign a form committing yourself to the transaction, although some funeral directors are prepared to come to your home. In most cases it will be, literally, just a signature: this is not a return to the dreaded bureaucracy.

You will not necessarily be expected to part with any money at this

stage, which may come as a considerable relief. Understandably,
however, the funeral home will want some evidence that you can pay
or that you are in a position to commit the family to this funeral. A
copy of the will, naming you as executor, will often suffice. You
might also consider acquiring a letter from your or the deceased's
bank manager stating that sufficient funds are available. If you are in
financial difficulty, be absolutely honest about this because there are
ways around the problem. You may feel tempted to book the funeral
and worry about the cost later, but this is creating unnecessary
anxiety for yourself (see Chapter 17). In no circumstances will the
deceased remain unburied. Funeral homes generally send an
account after the funeral has taken place.

## What next?

There are a number of things that must be done and decisions that
must be made, both by you and by the funeral director. Naturally, all
this needs to happen at virtually the same time. The order in which
you approach these tasks and decisions depends very much on the
circumstances of the death: your funeral director will advise you. In
the pages that follow, these tasks and decisions will be discussed in
detail to enable you see what needs to be done and what your
options are.

## ❶ Discuss All the Forms with the Funeral Director

You must make clear to the funeral director whether the body has
yet been released for burial, as legally he cannot collect the deceased
until the appropriate forms have been filled in. He absolutely must
be given the Green Form which the Registrar gave you. Other forms
will vary according to whether you want a burial or cremation, and
whether the coroner is involved or not (see Chapters 3 and 6). If you
are unsure about which forms you need, ask the funeral director for
help. He knows exactly what to do and can help you sort this out
without fuss or stress.

The most common situation in which the form-filling might not
yet have been completed is where the coroner has decided there is to
be a post-mortem. You will not know when his examination will be
completed and thus when the body can be released for burial. Don't
let this stop you making the initial arrangements for the funeral.

Do not feel like a fool or a time-waster if you are unsure of the
bureaucracy or you don't know when the body will be released. This
is exactly the kind of situation in which you can use the funeral
director's expertise which, after all, is what you are paying for.

## ⓣ Tell the Funeral Director Where the Body Is

The funeral director will arrange for the body to be collected and taken to the funeral home. He will usually use a coffin to transport the deceased, but under some circumstances will use a body bag.

If the deceased is in hospital, give the funeral director the name of the hospital and double check that you have given him the correct facts (name, etc) about the deceased. You should already have done this when you confirmed the arrangement, but it only takes a few seconds to run through the details again. This is especially important if the deceased's name is fairly common, like Smith.

Where the deceased is lying in another location, for example, at home, provide as much detail as possible about where exactly he is to be found. If, for example, he is in the top bedroom which can only be reached by a narrow winding staircase, the funeral director may decide it is impractical to use a coffin to transfer the deceased and instead use a body bag.

ⓗ     Try not to watch the body being taken away. It is distressing enough to see the coffin containing the deceased leaving the house, but even worse if the funeral director is forced to use a body bag.

## ⓣ Decide Whether You Want the Body Buried or Cremated

At some stage you are going to have to decide whether the deceased is to be buried or cremated.

### Burial

A site must be booked at the local cemetery or churchyard, if this has not already been done. The funeral director will liaise with the site to organize the gravediggers, and their fees will be added to your bill. The cemetery will have set hours in which burial is permitted, and are extremely unlikely to allow burials outside these times.

### Cremation

The time and date must be arranged with the crematorium and all the necessary paperwork completed. The funeral director will ensure that nothing remains in or on the body or coffin which is against the crematorium's rules. These rules are strict and may seem unreasonable, but they are based on environmental factors and on safety needs. Nothing can be incinerated which might give off noxious fumes, causing danger to the people in the immediate vicinity or to the atmosphere. When you remember that seventy per cent of the population is cremated, you can see that this could be a major problem if there were no regulations. Also, nothing can be permitted which might explode or otherwise endanger crematorium staff.

The funeral director will know these rules by heart and you can be certain he will permit nothing in the construction of the coffin which will break them. You must be honest with him about any electronic or artificial devices such as pacemakers in the deceased's body, as these are not permitted.

See Chapter 6 for a more detailed discussion of what is involved in a cremation.

### 🅣 Decide Whether You Want to View the Deceased

The funeral director will need to know whether the deceased's coffin is to be left open to allow friends and relatives to take one last look.

There is no norm that applies here. Some people regard the whole idea of viewing a body with revulsion, whereas others might be unable to accept the death until they have done so.

🅗   Take a box of handkerchiefs with you. Viewing a body can affect you even if you are normally very controlled.

There may also be other factors which apply. If, for example, the death occurred because of an accident, the funeral home might advise that viewing is inappropriate. They will not make the decision for you, but if there is considerable damage, it is their duty to warn you that the deceased might not appear as you would want to remember him.

🅗   In this situation you might want to ask them to cut a small lock of his hair for you to make the abruptness of the parting easier.

If you are certain the deceased is not to be viewed, tell the funeral director and he can seal the coffin almost immediately. However, don't feel pressured into making a decision. As with so many things relating to the funeral, you may not know your own mind until some time has elapsed. It might be wise to err on the side of caution and say that it should be assumed you will view unless and until you say otherwise. No one is going to force you to do so and you can always change your mind in the coming days. You do not have to make a final decision at this stage.

## What to expect

If you do decide to view the body, this will take place in the funeral home's Chapel of Rest. If you have never been in a Chapel of Rest before, you will find nothing there to upset you. The room is likely to be small and tastefully decorated, not large and intimidating, and will have the peaceful ambience of a place of worship. It is a good idea to tell the funeral director when you wish to view, as the staff can bring the deceased from the colder room where he is lying before your arrival and have him ready for you.

There is nothing, however, to stop you popping in unexpectedly. Grief takes people in different ways and it may be that, in the middle of doing something else, you are seized by a compulsive desire to see the deceased and to be with him for a few minutes. The funeral home should be happy to accommodate you, as long as it is within working hours.

In this situation, you will be asked to wait in a reception room for a few minutes while the necessary arrangements are being made. This can be distressing as you have time to sit and look around you, to realize that you are in a funeral home and that the death has indeed taken place. It is wise, however, to accept that these feelings are going to hit you anyway over the next few weeks and months: it is part of the grieving process. At least while you are waiting in the funeral home you know you are with caring and understanding people. It is, perhaps, a good environment in which to start the process of acceptance. It goes without saying that there should be no embarrassment whatsoever if you cry or rage. However you react, the funeral director will have seen it all before. If he couldn't cope with you and your grief, he would not be in the business.

Before you are shown into the Chapel of Rest the funeral director is likely to ask you if you would like him to remain with you. If you are pregnant or in ill health it might be wise to take him up on this offer: he will remain discreetly in the background, offering his support only if and when you need it. But if you feel you want to be alone with the deceased, say so. He will show you into the Chapel of Rest and then close the door to allow you your privacy.

What you will see is the deceased in his coffin which will be resting on a table or some other form of support. Unless you have specified otherwise, he will be dressed in a white funeral gown with only the head and hands visible. It is perfectly all right to touch or kiss the deceased. This can be extremely reassuring, although you should know that the body will feel cold. When you wish to leave, open the door and the funeral director will be waiting to escort you either to the exit or to a reception room if you are in tears and need time to recover.

You can visit more than once if you wish to, up until the time when the coffin is sealed before its journey to the church. The funeral director will tell you the last time when it is possible for you to visit.

## ❶ Set the Date for the Funeral

There are a number of factors you must consider here:

- The body must have been released for burial or cremation, and all the correct forms filled in.

- A time must be found in the funeral director's schedule: he will be arranging funerals for other people at the same time as helping you.

- The minister of religion must be free at that time to conduct the service.

- If there is to be a cremation, a time will have to be arranged with the crematorium.

- The date must be suitable for family and friends.

It is always wise to identify several possible days in case one of the other parties involved is not available at your preferred time.

All liaison with the minister of religion, the cemetery/ crematorium, and everyone else involved such as gravediggers, the organist, etc will be handled by the funeral director. All you have to do is tell him what you want.

## ❶ Decide Whether You Want the Body Embalmed

This is the subject that exercises a morbid fascination on people. There is often a feeling that, by agreeing to embalming, you are subjecting the deceased's body to an intrusive and degrading process which will turn him into a wax dummy. Many people also have a picture in their mind, gleaned mostly from horror movies, of blood being extracted from the body and rushing away through open gullies in the floor to drains.

The good news, which should come as no surprise when you think about it, is that medical science has moved on. Embalming is not a revolting and intrusive process, and the deceased is not going to be laid out on a table surrounded by a sea of blood.

The first fact you should know is that embalming is not required by the law. If you read the description below and still hate the very idea, no problem. Tell the funeral director you don't want it done.

Second, you should not be pressured by the funeral director to have the process carried out, although it must be said that some funeral homes insist on it. If they do – and this is a question you should ask when selecting a funeral home – you need to decide how you feel about this. If it is non-negotiable with them and you feel strongly about it, choose someone else. Remember that it is merely an option that is available.

## What is embalming?

It is the use of a preserving agent to delay the natural deterioration of a body. The effect lasts for roughly four or five weeks, so there is no danger of your turning the deceased into a wax dummy whose body will remain in the ground, gruesomely untouched, as the years pass.

As for the tubes and open gullies – forget it. These days the preserving fluid is inserted by injection into the deceased's arteries. It is as clean and simple as that.

## Why have the deceased embalmed?

You do not need to have it done, but there are advantages:

- Because of the colour of the fluid used, the deceased's skin will reacquire a slight pink tinge and thus look more natural. This can be helpful if the body is to be viewed, making the deceased look more as he did in life, which after all is how you want to remember him.

- Embalming is often known these days as 'hygienic treatment', which makes the deceased's body safer to handle and to be near. This is obviously better for you and for the staff at the funeral home. For the sake of one injection you are ensuring the health of everyone involved.

It is worth saying again that there is no legal obligation in most cases to have this done. The only time when it is obligatory is when the body has to be transported a long distance.

## ❶ Decide Whether You Want Cosmetics Used on the Body

This is a matter of personal choice. Many funeral homes will not use cosmetics unless specifically requested to do so, unlike in the United States, where it is almost standard practice. If, however, you feel this is desirable – perhaps because the deceased is a woman who, in life, would have hated to be seen without her makeup – tell the funeral director. If the deceased is a man, discuss the matter with the staff at the funeral home.

**H**    If the deceased is a woman, why not provide the funeral home with her own cosmetics? Any woman will tell you there are colours and brands that suit and others that don't. So the best solution may be to use cosmetics which the deceased herself preferred while she was alive.

## **T** Decide Whether You Want a Religious Ceremony, and Where

If you decide to hold a religious service you need to think about who is to conduct that service, and what it is to consist of. You have several options. You can:

- Hold the service in a place of worship.
- Hold a service at the graveside.
- Use the crematorium chapel if the deceased is being cremated.

You need to ensure that the person you wish to conduct the service is free to do so on that date. Also, if you want input into the design of the service, you must allow yourself time to see the minister and discuss your needs. You should remember that if you want an organist, he also must be told in advance.

## **T** Discuss Any Religious Requirements with the Funeral Director

Learning about the funeral requirements for different faiths forms an important part of a funeral director's training, so do not feel diffident about approaching a funeral home owned by Christians if you are, say, a Muslim or a Hindu. He will know exactly what is required and should be able to provide it.

## **T** Choose Flowers and Cards

When you are organizing a funeral it is entirely up to you whether mourners are allowed to express their grief by sending flowers or whether you'd prefer to name a charity to which they can send donations.

You might wish to send flowers yourself – a wreath, or a display. Clearly, cost will be a factor but there might be flowers that meant a great deal to the deceased: perhaps he was particularly fond of roses and grew them in his garden, or freesias were included in a bridal bouquet in years past. Also, these days florists can fashion flowers into words, such as MUM, or into a name or pet name. Undoubtedly, flowers add a touch of colour and life into a sad event and it is one way for the bereaved to express their love for the deceased.

The cost is likely to vary enormously, but you will be lucky to pay less than £15 for the simplest display or wreath: obviously, more complex arrangements will cost considerably more.

You do, of course, have the option of going to a local florist, but many funeral directors will have a catalogue issued either by a local shop or by a large chain which shows pictures of displays and wreaths, together with a price list. This is worth considering as it means one less journey for you, and the funeral director can take charge of the ordering and ensure your choice is delivered to the right place on the right day. He will also be able to help any other mourners who wish to order through him.

You will also probably find that the funeral director has a range of 'in memoriam' cards for you to attach to the wreath or bouquet. These will have a tasteful design in the corner and words such as 'To Mum' or 'Deepest Regrets' written on them. You can write your message and the funeral director will ensure that the card is attached to the correct floral arrangement.

It may be that you feel money spent on flowers is wasted, considering the number of reputable charities in urgent need of money. You can decide to request all mourners to send donations to a named charity in lieu of flowers, and many people choose to do this.

## ❶ Arrange Notices in the Press if Required

Even if the deceased led a relatively isolated life it is always worth considering placing a notice in the 'Deaths' column of the local paper. This is particularly useful if the deceased had lived in the area for some time. There may be people to whom he was once close but had lost contact with over the years who would wish to pay their last respects.

If the deceased had friends or professional contacts over a wider geographical area, you might wish to consider placing a notice in one of the major national papers.

You can, of course, do this yourself. If so, you might want to use one of the sample notices in Appendix 1. If you prefer, however, you can hand this matter over to the funeral director. It saves you tracking down copies of the relevant papers for their addresses, phoning to find out their rates and sending in your notice. Many people find it easier to work with the funeral director to create the correct wording and leave the rest to him. You can use a message in the newspapers to state whether you want flowers or not.

In the past, placing a notice in the 'Deaths' column was the only way to spread the news of a death. These days many people talk to one another via their computers, using the Internet. It is a slightly unusual suggestion, but it might be worth checking whether the deceased was interested in computers and used the Internet: a surprising number of people do. Often, such people never meet but discuss shared interests via their screens and quite meaningful 'computer friendships' can develop. If you think the deceased might have used the Internet, you might consider sending a notice of the death to his friends using this system, provided you can find their computer addresses (which are quite different from their real addresses). It is quite possible that this is the only way you will be able to reach them, as the deceased may well not have their real addresses or even their real names. This is something of a specialist area and this book is not the place to teach you in detail about computers. The best thing to do is to look in Yellow Pages for a local computer shop and explain the problem to them. Most of these shops are staffed by enthusiasts who are generally very helpful.

### ❶ Consider Transport for the Mourners

The coffin will, of course, be transported by hearse. You can arrange, via the funeral director, for bearers to lift and carry it, so this is not a problem you have to deal with. The more difficult decision is how much transport to arrange for friends and mourners. It is sensible to arrange a limousine for the immediate family, and this will often be included in the overall cost of the funeral. However, often one limousine will not be enough. You need to balance the cost of hiring further limousines against the needs and sensitivities of other mourners. Points you might want to consider are:

- Their closeness to the deceased. It might seem reasonable to hire a second car for other family members and the deceased's closest friends, but you might feel that Aunty Maud, who hardly ever spoke a civil word to the deceased when he was alive, should make her own arrangements or travel in a taxi organized (at far less cost than a limousine) by the funeral director.

- The emotional state of the mourner. If someone is likely to be totally distraught, is it fair to ask them to drive in that condition, or be driven by an indifferent taxi driver?

- The overall health of some of the mourners, particularly the elderly. The funeral will be an ordeal for them even if they were not close to the deceased, because of their own age. Can they cope with finding the right taxi after the interment?

- The parking situation if there is a church service. Many churches have their own car park but this is not always the case in inner city areas.

These are things only you can decide, as the funeral director will not know the mourners.

If you are going to hire additional limousines or taxis, you should give the funeral director as much notice as possible. Be aware that many funeral directors will do more than this if necessary, such as arranging a mini-bus to pick up people from a station or airport. The decision as to who travels in which form of transport is yours, but you can hand the actual organization over to the funeral director.

### ● Decide Whether You Want to Offer Refreshments After the Funeral

Many people like to organize food and drink for after the funeral. It provides an opportunity for mourners to express their regrets and for everyone to swap memories of the deceased. It can also be an excellent way of giving the immediate family something to do after the funeral instead of going home to a horribly empty house. This is entirely a matter for personal preference: some people can't afford to do this or don't want to. However, in some cultures it is almost obligatory. It may be that preparing the food is a useful way of keeping immediate family occupied in the days before the funeral but if you feel they cannot cope, it is worth asking the funeral director if he will organize catering. Many are prepared to do this.

### ● Decide What to Wear

Don't leave this until the last moment: you may have nothing suitable and need to go out and buy something, or you may need to have an outfit dry-cleaned.

Wear something you are comfortable in. The last thing you need on the day of the funeral is to be worrying whether the button at your waist is going to burst because you have put on a few pounds since you last wore the garment.

Hats used to be obligatory at funerals, but this is less true these days. They are useful, however, if you feel you want to shield your face from prying eyes. Sunglasses are also helpful, especially at the graveside or immediately after the cremation, when you might be in tears.

## ❶ Decide If You Want Any Special Arrangements Made

As you will have realized by now, all funerals are to some extent designer funerals and it is not at all the conveyor-belt system you might have imagined.

However, if you can do more to make the funeral exactly as you think it should be, and as long as it is legal the funeral director should be prepared to carry out your wishes.

Some of the more common ideas are:

- Burying items of special meaning or sentimental value with the deceased.

- Having the hearse travel to the interment via the deceased's favourite walk, or past his favourite pub or football ground.

- Arranging to have the deceased dressed in an outfit of particular importance, such as military uniform or a wedding gown.

Whatever it is, if it gives you comfort and seems right in the circumstances, no matter how bizarre it might seem to others, you should feel free to ask if your wishes can be accommodated.

### Order of Events

There is no absolutely set order of events because so many factors can vary. The deceased might have died in hospital after a long illness, having specifically requested burial. This means that the certification process is easy, no post-mortem is required, you know you need to arrange a burial, and the date for the funeral can be set immediately. In other circumstances the deceased might have been the victim of a road accident, requiring a post-mortem, and if cremation is desired, needing certification by two doctors. This means a wait before the date of the funeral can be set.

There may be other factors involved: perhaps the funeral has to wait until an important mourner can travel from abroad. Nevertheless, there is a rough order in which you should consider things which will help the funeral director give you the best possible service.

# 5

# The Hole in the Ground

If it has been decided that the deceased is to be buried rather than cremated, one of the first things you must check is whether a burial plot has already been arranged and if so, where it is. It is often possible for someone to arrange a burial plot for themselves, and perhaps for their partner, while the are still alive and you should consider whether the deceased has already attended to this. If, after checking, you find that the deceased hasn't done so, a plot needs to be arranged as a matter of urgency.

## ❶ Check to See if a Plot Has Already Been Arranged

This is a relatively easy process because there are only a limited number of places for you to look, and you can work by a process of elimination.

### What to look for and where to look

Anyone who arranges a plot should acquire some evidence of the transaction. Exactly what this looks like depends on the cemetery or churchyard with which he has dealt. Assume that you are looking for either some kind of deed or receipt, usually one page in length, with a reference number detailing the location of the grave and the name of the cemetery.

The deceased should have kept the written evidence of the transaction safely among his papers. You cannot, however, assume this as some people are chronically allergic to paperwork and lose even the most important documents. This should not prove a barrier to finding out exactly what the situation is. The places you should look are:

- Among the deceased's papers for a contract, receipt or deed. Most people keep their important documents together, so it is likely that the information will be lodged with, for example, the deeds to the house or the deceased's passport. You might also, if the deceased was elderly, check to see whether he made use of one of Age Concern's helpful forms on which useful information can be recorded.

(H)   If your family has used one particular funeral director in the past, ask him if he has any useful knowledge about this. If someone has had to arrange a funeral before, he may have taken the opportunity to arrange a plot for himself at the same time.

- On the deceased's computer. Many people who are not themselves at ease with computers do not realize the extent to which the computer-literate use them to store information. If the deceased had a computer, check to see if there are housekeeping files containing information such as addresses or contacts. If so, search through all of these and you may well find some reference to the grave that will help you.

- Check to see if there is a reference number and the name of the churchyard or cemetery scribbled anywhere: the deceased might have made a separate note of this when he made the transaction. Good places to search are at the front or back of a diary, an address book or in any notebooks you find.

(H)   As long as there is a record of the deceased having purchased the grave, it does not usually matter if you can't produce the actual document. All you have to do is to prove you are a relative of the deceased and are involved in arranging the funeral.

- If the deceased practised one of the more widespread religions, such as Methodism, Catholicism or was a member of the Church of England, he might have arranged a burial site in a local church graveyard. Sit down with the telephone directory and phone each of the churches, asking if their records contain his name.

(H)   While you are on the phone ask for a list of churches of that faith which have graveyards – not all do. This will save wasted phone calls.

- If the deceased was a member of a faith other than the Church of England, phone a minister of religion of that faith, or your funeral director, and ask them if there is a cemetery dedicated to members of that religion near to where the deceased lived. If so, phone them up, explain your problem, give them the deceased's details and ask them to check their records.

- Phone the 'Cemeteries' department of the local authority. You should be able to find their direct number from the telephone directory but be aware that sometimes cemeteries are part of a larger department, such as Parks or Environmental Health, and there may not be a specific listing for them. In this situation, phone the General Enquiries line and ask them to put you through: it is time-wasting to try to guess where 'Cemeteries' might be hidden.

  Ask them for a list of all the cemeteries owned and run by the local authority: they should also be able to give you details of any private cemeteries in the area. Having got this list, phone each of them and check whether they have had dealings with the deceased.

If you have tried all these avenues of approach and failed to find a plot registered in the deceased's name, you can safely assume that he did not make advance arrangements for his burial. You must therefore go ahead and acquire a plot on his behalf.

### ❶ Decide Where You Want the Deceased Buried

This should be a straightforward matter that can be settled easily, although there are a few potential problems which will be discussed later.

Before you start your search for a site, there are several points you should consider:

- Check to see whether the deceased himself has left any stated preference, eg in his will (see page 131).

- Do you want to organize this yourself or do you want to hand the task over to your funeral director? If you do, check to see whether he will charge extra for this job (many will not). Even so, it might be worthwhile as it will certainly save you some work.

- Where do you want the deceased to be buried? You

theoretically have the choice of:
- A local churchyard.
- A local authority cemetery.
- A private cemetery.
- A denominational cemetery (one exclusively for people of a particular faith).

In fact, your choice might be slightly more limited, but more of that later.

- If you have not already done so, get a list of all the cemeteries in the area from the local authority, and of the churches of the deceased's faith which have graveyards. You will then need to consider:

  - Distance: If family are likely to want to visit the grave, how difficult the journey is likely to be.
  - Religion: Are you happy with a non-denominational cemetery or would it be preferable to bury the deceased in one dedicated to his religion? Some non-denominational cemeteries, in fact, have sections dedicated to people of a particular faith.
  - Upkeep of cemetery: You will not know whether the cemetery is well maintained unless you visit, but you may wish to do so. Visiting a cemetery also has the advantage of showing you what peaceful places they are.

It might be useful to look at some of these points in greater detail.

As already explained, you may have the choice of a number of burial sites – local authority cemeteries, denominational cemeteries and churchyards.

## Churchyards

In theory, anyone who lives or dies within a parish has a right to be buried in the church graveyard. This has been a longstanding tradition – perhaps too longstanding, because so many people have taken advantage of this over the years that most churchyards are now full up.

You need to contact your local vicar or priest and he will be able to tell you immediately whether space is available or not.

## Cemeteries

### Local authority cemeteries

Each local council owns and runs cemeteries. These days some cemeteries are run on a day-to-day basis by private firms but the land is still owned by the local authority.

The good news is that you will, by phoning around, almost certainly be able to find space somewhere for the deceased in a local cemetery. What is more, the procedure for acquiring a space is usually quite simple.

The bad news is that cemeteries are filling up fast. You will find a space, but it may not be in your first choice of resting place. Many cemeteries, particularly in inner cities, are already full and burials are taking place in sites on the edge of town.

Most local authority cemeteries are non-denominational: as long as there is space, the deceased can find a final resting place there, regardless of the faith he followed during his life. However, the faith which the deceased followed in life may be of considerable importance to his family, and indeed to the deceased himself prior to his death, and this has been taken into account, where possible, by the local authorities. In many, but not all, local authority cemeteries there is an area for the specific use of people from a particular faith. The ground has been consecrated to that religion and only people of that faith can be buried there. A quick phone call to the Cemeteries Department will tell you whether this is so in your area.

## Denominational cemeteries

There may be a cemetery in your area dedicated exclusively to a particular faith. This is most likely in areas where there is a large concentration of members of one faith, and of course some places of worship may have land attached to the place of worship which is used as a burial ground.

Obviously, you will have to prove that the deceased was a member of the appropriate faith. You may find that some cemeteries are stricter than others about this: one cemetery might, for example, feel that a lifetime ignoring the faith into which the deceased was born disqualifies him from burial there. The majority, however, are much less rigid and as long as there is space you should have no problems.

## Availability of space

You may have heard stories about how it is now impossible to bury the dead in certain parts of the country due to lack of space. These stories can be very upsetting as you obviously want to do the right thing by the deceased, and there may be strong reasons for not wanting to consider cremation. It is true that there is a space problem, but fortunately the situation is not yet that grim, and some areas of the country are not yet affected at all.

Cemeteries in large towns and cities are often now either full or nearly full. In this situation the local authority either commissions a new cemetery on land it already owns, or it acquires land on the edge of town. Sometimes, arrangements are made with other, nearby local authorities to bury the dead in their area.

The important point to remember is that at the moment, local authorities are finding ways to cope with this lack of space. It is possible you may have to travel to visit the grave, but even so, this is not likely to be unreasonably far, and you may be lucky enough to live in an area where the problem has not yet reached that stage.

Probably the most useful person you can ask for information and help with this problem is your funeral director. As he handles burials almost every day, he will know exactly what the situation is and where space is available.

You might be interested to know that most local authorities see this lack of space as a major problem for the future. Quite simply, in years to come, other solutions to the problem are going to have to be found.

**(H)**   If you live in a city which has this problem you might want to consider where you yourself want to be buried, and purchase space for yourself locally while it is still available. Be warned that the cemetery is almost certain to charge you more for this.

## **(T) Decide What Type of Grave You Want**

You might be surprised to learn that you have a choice in the matter, but you do. It is a common assumption that each body has exclusive use of his or her own grave but in fact, this is not so: it is a privilege you have to pay for. Unless you do, other bodies can be buried on top of the deceased at a later stage. You have the choice between two types of grave: exclusive (or private) and non-exclusive (or public).

### Private graves

When you pay for a private site you are not buying the land from the church or local authority, but paying for the right to bury the deceased in that plot. Exclusive graves are sometimes known as private graves, and this describes them accurately. The grave is 'private' to the person buried in it, and by arrangement, any other named person. This right will exist for a specific number of years, but not indefinitely. The period varies from cemetery to cemetery, but is usually between twenty-five and seventy-five years. After that, unless you pay for an extension to your right to exclusivity (which might not always be allowed), that right ends and others may be buried in that grave without your knowledge or consent.

## Non-exclusive graves

These are sometimes known as public graves. Here, you acquire the right to bury the deceased in a grave which may, at some stage, possibly quite soon, contain others. You don't know who will be buried there and you don't know when. Because of this the cost of the grave is considerably less.

Different places have different policies on this. Some guarantee that no one else will be buried in that grave for a specific number of years (but, of course, a shorter period of time than if you had purchased a private grave). Other places make no such guarantee, and another person may be interred there almost immediately.

Some people find this idea immensely disturbing, almost sacrilegious. Others find it irrelevant, believing that as long as the remains are not disturbed, the policy is perfectly acceptable.

**ⓗ** Find out the price of both public and private before you make a decision. If you set your heart on a private grave and then find you can't afford it, you may be upset that you have to opt for a public grave.

Some older people will be familiar with the term 'Pauper's Grave'. It comes from the days when poor people, unable to provide a decent funeral for their deceased family member, were forced to rely on the authorities to arrange a grave site. In those days, the bare minimum was provided, and this was a cause of great distress. If you have very little money you might fear that this is what will happen to you or to your loved ones. Don't worry: things have changed. You can put away all thoughts of anonymous pits dug in the ground.

A public grave is not just a new name for the old pauper's grave. These days, all people are interred with dignity, and if you choose a public grave you will still have a grave site to visit, and where you can erect a tribute to the deceased if you wish (see Chapter 8).

Also, under some circumstances local authorities have a duty to bury someone who has died (see page 175). Again, this does not mean the deceased will get a pauper's funeral. All it means is that the local authority bears the cost of a proper burial in a public grave.

## Non-disturbance of graves

It is very important to know that the remains of the first person buried in a grave are absolutely never, under any circumstances, disturbed by the burial of a second person in the same grave, whether the grave is private or public.

Each grave, public or private, is dug deeply enough to allow for the burial of a second person: the average depth of a grave is seven feet. The gravediggers will always ensure that two feet of earth separate the two.

In some cemeteries, if you purchase a private grave you can arrange for it to be deeper than this, although of course that will cost extra. This is to allow more than two people to be buried there – perhaps the spouse of the deceased and their child. You do, however, need to discuss this with the person in charge before the grave is dug and the first person interred.

If you are thinking about acquiring a public grave, don't forget that it is not just the wishes of the deceased you need to consider. Relatives left behind, especially a spouse or partner, must live with the fact that the deceased's final resting place may be disturbed during their lifetime. If they cannot cope with this idea, you should not do anything, if at all possible, that will add to their distress.

Points to consider

There are four points it might be useful to consider when faced with the choice between a public and private grave:

- Obviously, the wishes of the deceased and his family must be taken into account.

- The cost – a private grave is more expensive than a public one.

- The length of the exclusivity agreement. If it is for say, seventy-five years, most existing friends and relatives will themselves have died when the contract for exclusive use of the grave expires. If you are only offered a shorter period, say twenty-five years or less, you need to consider whether the difference between exclusivity and non-exclusivity is long enough to make it worth paying for.

- The age of those left behind. If all the deceased's friends and relatives are elderly and unlikely to survive for many more years, would it be a kindness even to explain the difference between public and private graves to them if they don't already know, or would it upset them? Don't forget, this is something that will shortly affect them.

🅣 Deal with the Bureaucracy of Acquiring a Grave

This is easy – you decide what you want, and someone else fills in all the papers.

## Local Authority Cemeteries

You can either:

- Go in person to the cemetery and deal direct with the staff on site (this isn't always encouraged); or

- Ask your funeral director to act as intermediary. Some people can't face the thought of seeing a cemetery immediately after a death.

### Can you choose the actual site?

Yes, if it is a private grave. Again, policy on this differs from cemetery to cemetery, but you may be offered different sites at different prices. The kind of thing that might affect the price is, for example, the nearness of the site to a path.

Staff usually encourage you to visit the cemetery in person to view the site before making your mind up. In this way you will be able to see exactly what it is you are purchasing. You might, for example, find the site next to a path which, although it sounded ideal on paper is, in fact, too public, so the passage of people to and fro might intrude on your privacy when you visit.

**ⓗ**   If you are uneasy about visiting the cemetery to make your choice, why not take the opportunity to walk round and look at the different headstones and memorials, and the inscriptions they bear? This will help you decide whether you want to erect one later and what it might say. It will also help you understand that you can still do something for the deceased after the funeral is over.

As for public graves, again, policy will differ on this, but in general you will not be able to choose the site.

### Paperwork

If you have opted for a private grave, what usually happens is that the cemetery manager, or one of his staff, will check the records to see what is available and where it is. When you have made your choice, you will receive a grant of that site. This grant is a piece of paper documenting the fact that you have bought the private use of that grave for a specific number of years.

In the case of a public grave, you will receive a sheet of paper recording the fact that the deceased is to be buried in a particular grave and this document will give you the reference number of that grave.

## Church Graveyards

If you are lucky enough to find a churchyard with space available, you need to decide whether you want exclusivity or non-exclusivity, as discussed above. The procedures for the two are quite different.

If space is available and you don't want private use, it is very simple. The vicar (not you) will allocate a spot and the funeral can go ahead.

If you want to purchase the private use of the plot there is a process you must go through which is slightly archaic but nothing to worry about as most of the work is done by someone else.

Ask the vicar or priest for the address of the diocesan registrar, a slightly daunting title for the administrator of an area including that parish. You write to him saying that you wish to buy the right to bury someone in the churchyard. He will do some research and, after a few weeks, will grant you a licence to bury a particular person in a spot which they (not you) will designate. The fee will depend on the amount of work they have to do.

Obviously, this rather drawn-out procedure is impractical in situations where you have not considered the matter beforehand. You can hardly be expected to leave the deceased in the funeral home for six or seven weeks while the diocesan registrar goes through administrative formalities. Don't worry. Simply ask the vicar or priest to allocate a spot as if you did not want exclusive rights, carry on with the funeral, then apply to the diocesan registrar for exclusive right to use this plot for other members of the family. Therefore, even though the plot did not start out by being exclusive, it ends up that way.

### ❶ Decide Whether This Grave is to Contain More Than One Person: If So, How Many?

If the deceased has a husband, wife, partner or children still living, they may want to consider being buried in the same grave site as the deceased when their times come, thus ensuring that they remain together in death. This, of course, means you must pay for a private grave, but you will then have the right to decide who else is buried there. A grave is usually able to accommodate two people: if you think more will wish to be buried in the same site, arrange for the original grave to be dug deeper (see page 51).

### ❶ Decide Whether You Want Cremated Ashes Buried

Everything that has been said applies, of course, to the burial of ashes in a cemetery or churchyard. You go about acquiring a site in exactly the same manner. Cremation is discussed as a separate topic in Chapter 6.

### 🅣 Make Sure You Know What it Will All Cost

Costs will vary enormously from one cemetery to another, but be prepared for something of a shock: purchasing a private grave is not cheap. You should expect to pay at least £100 and often very much more than that for a private grave, and £100 to £200 for a public grave.

On top of this, there will be the cost of having the grave dug.

You will almost certainly be charged more – as much as fifty per cent extra – if you live outside the normal catchment area for that cemetery.

In the case of a churchyard burial, costs vary too much for an estimate to be meaningful.

# 6

# Cremation

Cremation is an option that should be considered as early as possible after the death as there are special forms to fill in and this may take a little time. At first sight, the number of forms involved in a cremation might seem daunting, but the good news is that in many cases someone else has to fill them in. There are some forms you might never even get to see. You should, however, know what is involved so that if someone asks you, for example, whether Forms B and C have been filled in yet, you know what they are talking about.

## Who can be cremated?

The only major religious groups which forbid cremation are Orthodox Jews and Muslims. Every other major religion permits cremation, and for some it is obligatory. Cremation was previously forbidden for Catholics but this ban was lifted in 1963: most Catholics now find it perfectly acceptable. You may find, however, that older Catholics who were accustomed to the pre-1963 situation may still object to cremation for their relatives and this is a situation that must be handled with some care.

## ❶ Remember to Register the Death

Don't forget that you have to register the death in exactly the same way as for a burial (see Chapter 3). The forms you need to take are discussed below.

## ❶ Tackle the Bureaucracy Needed for a Cremation

You will not be terribly surprised by now to learn that there are different forms to be filled in, depending on whether the coroner is involved or not.

- If the coroner is *not* called in, you will need Forms A,B,C and F. The last three are all filled in by doctors.

- If the coroner *is* called in there is one less form to bother with. Forms B and C are no longer necessary: instead, the coroner fills in Form E.

- You will also need to sign a form about the disposal of the ashes.

- Before the funeral the crematorium will provide a form confirming the date of the cremation.

- After the funeral the crematorium will produce yet another form confirming that it took place.

This all sounds very daunting but it is not, because most of the work is going to be done by someone else. All these forms will be discussed in detail below so that you know exactly what is going on and what you, yourself, have to do (not very much).

## Do I have to get all these forms signed myself?

Not if you have a funeral director, no. He will do all the hard work. There will only be one form that you have to deal with personally, but more of that later.

 Tell the funeral director as soon as possible that you want a cremation to take place to give him time to do this.

Hopefully, your funeral director will obtain all the forms for you, but in case you want to do it yourself, or to help you understand what is going on, you should know you get them either from the funeral director *or* the crematorium.

To prevent you becoming totally confused, the forms you need to have signed have been divided into two batches:

- Those you need for the cremation to go ahead at all;
and
- Those which confirm various arrangements.

## The 'Go Ahead' Forms

### Form A (application for cremation)

On this form you are asking for the crematorium to cremate the deceased. It is all very straightforward. If you get the form from the funeral director you can ask him to sit by you while you fill it in.

This form has to be signed by two people:

- Either the next of kin or the executor; and

- A householder who knows that person.

This last one sounds a bit tricky on the surface, but what almost invariably happens is that the funeral director provides the second signature.

### Forms B and C (medical forms)

These have to be signed by doctors.

The reason why you must have two forms signed by doctors for a cremation, but only one for a burial, is common sense. In theory, no person can be buried or cremated unless the cause of death is absolutely clear (see Chapter 3). However, you will know from reading the papers and watching the news on TV that occasionally the courts will order a body to be exhumed in the light of new evidence about the death. This, of course, is not possible when the body has been cremated; therefore the state is making doubly sure that the cause of death is known and agreed on by two different doctors.

Form B must be signed by the doctor who treated the deceased during the last illness. He must personally examine the body after the death.

Form C also needs to be signed by a doctor. This doctor must:

- Have been registered as a doctor in the United Kingdom for five years or more (be well qualified):

- Be able to act as an independent medical opinion:

  – He must not be a partner of the doctor who signed Form B:

  – He must be unrelated either to the deceased or to the doctor who signed Form B.

What this means in practical terms is that if, for example, the deceased's GP signs Form B, you cannot ask a partner in that practice to sign Form C. Nor can you ask the deceased's brother, if he happens to be a doctor, to sign.

When the deceased dies in hospital the requirements are even more stringent. The doctors who sign Forms B and C must have worked on different wards and one of them must not have treated the deceased.

The doctor signing Form C has, of course, to see the body before signing.

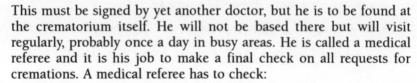

**(H)** You may wonder if you are going to have problems finding a second doctor to sign. Perhaps you have visions of yourself desperately ringing round all the GPs in the area trying to find a volunteer. You couldn't be more wrong. First, the funeral director will handle all this if you ask him to. He will know all the local GPs, and also the right people to contact inside the hospital. He will have done this a thousand times. Second, the doctors who sign Forms B and C are paid for doing so (by you, but this will go on the funeral director's bill). As you can imagine, this is something of an incentive for them to assist you.

So although there is an extra form to be signed by a doctor, it is not going to cause a difficulty. Clearly, though, you are going to have to allow time for this to be done, and that is one of the reasons for needing to decide on cremation as early as possible.

When the coroner is involved, Forms B and C are no longer needed. Instead he will issue a certificate for cremation, known as Form E.

**(H)** If the coroner is involved, don't forget to tell him if the deceased is to be cremated, so that he can fill in the correct form (there is a separate form the coroner can fill in for a burial). Don't wait until the end of the investigation.

### Form F

This must be signed by yet another doctor, but he is to be found at the crematorium itself. He will not be based there but will visit regularly, probably once a day in busy areas. He is called a medical referee and it is his job to make a final check on all requests for cremations. A medical referee has to check:

- To see that all the necessary signatures have been collected:

- That the information on the form is correct (he will, for example, check the stated cause of death):

- That everything conforms to the regulations governing cremation (for example, that the deceased isn't still wearing a pacemaker).

### Who gets which form

It really is far easier if you let the funeral director handle all this. If you do, the only form you need deal with directly before the cremation is Form A, which you might need to sign as the next of kin or executor, or arrange for someone else to sign. The remaining forms can be distributed between the doctors, the crematorium and your funeral director, and you need never even see them.

As mentioned, the coroner will sign Form E. You will get the pink copy and it is this you take to the Registrar to register the death. The coroner will send Form E directly to your funeral director. He in turn will pass this to the crematorium, so you will not need to concern yourself with it.

## Forms Confirming Arrangements

There are three more forms needed, only one of which directly involves you.

### Disposal of Ashes form

At some stage, while all these above-mentioned forms are flying between the doctors, your funeral director and the crematorium, you might be asked to sign a form saying exactly what you want done with the ashes.

It is important for you to understand that you do not have to sign this form immediately. Don't be rushed into a decision. Talk it over with anyone else involved before signing.

You may be unsure exactly what you want done with the ashes after the cremation, or you may still be trying to arrange a grave for them at the local cemetery if they can't be buried in the crematorium grounds. Whatever the reason, if you are not absolutely sure what you want done with the ashes after the ceremony, don't sign. There is no pressure on you to do so, as you can make this decision after the cremation, if necessary. Give yourself time to think things over if you need it.

### Certificate for Disposal of Cremated Remains

This is a form that the crematorium produces, stating that the remains can now be buried in a cemetery or churchyard if you so wish.

### Certificate of Cremation for Burial or Scattering

This again is produced by the crematorium, and is a statement that the cremation has taken place. This will go to the person who signed Form A (the executor or next of kin).

### Who gets which form?

Having described all these forms in some detail, it might be useful to look at them again briefly to see who does what and who gets what.

## Where no coroner

| Form | Purpose | Signed by | Given to |
|---|---|---|---|
| Form A | Application for cremation | Executor or next of kin | Crematorium |
| Form B | States cause of death | Doctor | Crematorium (medical referee) |
| Form C | States cause of death | Doctor | Crematorium (medical referee) |
| Form F | Says everything in order | Medical referee | Crematorium |
| Ashes Disposal Form | What is to be done with ashes | You | Crematorium |
| Certificate for Disposal of Cremated Remains | Confirms arrangements | Crematorium | |
| Certificate of cremation for burial or scattering | States cremation carried out | Crematorium | Executor/ next of kin |

## Where coroner involved

As mentioned, you have one less form to deal with here. Many of the others are exactly the same.

| Form | Purpose | Signed by | Given to |
|---|---|---|---|
| Form A | Application for cremation | Executor or next of kin | Crematorium |
| Form E | Replaces Forms B and C | Coroner | Crematorium (medical referee) |
| Form F | Says everything in order | Medical referee | Crematorium |
| Ashes Disposal Form | What is to be done with ashes | You | Crematorium |
| Certificate for Disposal of Cremated Remains | Confirms arrangements | Crematorium | |
| Certificate of cremation for burial or scattering | States cremation carried out | Crematorium | Executor/ next of kin |

You will see from the list opposite that you are very rarely mentioned. Forms will pass between various people via your funeral director and apart from ensuring things are done, you can let other people handle it. Regarded in that light, it doesn't t seem too bad.

## ❶ Decide Whether You Want to Hold a Service and Where

Many people now opt for a service in the crematorium chapel. This will almost invariably be a non-denominational chapel open for use by most religions. The service can be conducted by a minister provided by the crematorium or by one you yourself select. This includes Catholic priests and, in some cases, rabbis from the Reform Jewish community.

If the deceased or your family is not religious you can often have the service conducted by someone from the Secular Society or Humanists (see Appendix 5) or, sometimes, by a member of the crematorium staff.

It is, however, perfectly in order to hold the service elsewhere, for example, in your local parish church. You might, in this case, want a short committal ceremony in the crematorium chapel to allow a few words to be said as the deceased is removed for cremation.

### The crematorium chapel

Almost every crematorium has a chapel attached. As it is used solely for cremation services you should be prepared for it to seem slightly more impersonal than a church. Churches have a certain feel about them which comes from their being used by a regular congregation for a variety of services, some happy and some sad. Crematoria, on the other hand, are places few people visit more than once or twice in their lifetime, so they lack the continuity of use by the same group of people and their sole function is to allow services for the dead. If you are a regular churchgoer you might find the difference in atmosphere particularly noticeable. If you are not, you might find the non-denominational nature of the chapel's interior more acceptable than the inside of a church. Whatever your religious views you will see nothing to upset you.

## ❶ Decide If You Want There to be a Religious Service

You have the right to ask for a short service held in the chapel. You can request a minister of religion of your choice to hold the service: this can be arranged by you or by the funeral director. You will be allocated a certain amount of time in which to hold the service, usually twenty minutes, but in that period the service can take any form agreed upon by the deceased's family and the minister. This means you can have any prayers or hymns you think are appropriate, and you can arrange for the minister to speak about the deceased, exactly as if you were in a church. Many crematorium chapels have some facility for music. Check exactly what they can offer. Some may have an organ, in which case you can choose your own music. Others may have suitable pre-recorded music.

### ❶ If You Want a Non-Religious Service, Decide Who Will Hold It

The preceding pages have assumed that there will be some religious element to the cremation and this is true for the majority of people, in some cases because the deceased had strong religious beliefs, in other cases solely to comfort elderly relatives or others close to the deceased. However, these days a sizeable minority are actively opposed to introducing a religious element into the service and it is, of course, absolutely right that they should have this option. At a moment of great distress, why should grieving friends and relatives have a religion in which they don't believe thrust upon them? Crematoria throughout the country recognize and accept this. Those wishing for a non-religious service often approach either the British Humanist Association or National Secular Society. Both addresses are given Appendix 5.

What is crucial is that the service, whatever form it takes, should be appropriate to the deceased and offer comfort to friends and relatives. If any attempt is made to influence you towards holding a religious service you do not want, ignore it.

No venue can allow services for the dead to extend indefinitely as there will be other calls on their time. One main difference between holding a service in a church and in a crematorium chapel is that in most cases you will be allocated less time and the service cannot be allowed to overrun. You need to check this carefully as it varies from place to place. It can be as little as twenty minutes, it can be as much as forty-five minutes and, in some places, you can pay for additional time. You will need to know exactly how much time you have as soon as possible in order to design a service. It is also essential to remember that the time limits must be strictly adhered to.

The reason why is easy to understand and remembering it will help on the day as the service draws to a close: outside the crematorium, another family will be arriving in their cars. They, like you, want things to go smoothly. If they were forced to hang around outside the chapel, it would be extremely distressing for them. When you think of it this way, it is easier to accept the rather brutal fact that you have your allotted time in the chapel, and that is that. The amount of time you are allowed is something you can establish very early on in a quick phone call to the crematorium, even before you have obtained the necessary signatures on Forms A, B, C and F.

## ⓣ Make Sure You Know Exactly What Happens at a Cremation

If you have chosen a religious service, it will be very similar to one held in a church. If you are not sure what is involved in a Christian ceremony, see Chapter 4. There may also be a book containing the words of the service for each person in the chapel. The main difference comes at the end of the ceremony.

You are in the crematorium chapel and the service is drawing to a close. The coffin bearing the remains of the deceased is on the catafalque with a screen or a curtain in front of it. The minister will have spoken a few words about the deceased and you will have said a few prayers or perhaps sung a hymn. He will then say something like 'we consign our dearly beloved (name) to the ashes', he will discreetly press a handle or pull a lever, the curtains will draw, hiding the coffin from view and it will slide gently away, possibly with a slight whir of machinery. This is, of course, the most heart-rending part of the service and a certain amount of distress is inevitable, as in the moment when a coffin is laid in the ground for a burial. However, considerable care is taken to ensure that you don't see exactly what happens after that. It is possible the minister will ask you to pray in silence for a few minutes, but at this point the service is effectively at an end. Then, you and the other family and friends will file out of the chapel, where you can look quietly at any floral tributes that have been sent as tributes to the deceased. You might also want to look at the Book of Remembrance, or any plaques, to see if this is something you want to do for the deceased.

Where possible, the actual cremation will take place immediately after the service.

## ⓣ Arrange to Collect and Dispose of the Ashes

You can usually arrange to collect the ashes the next day. You have a surprising freedom as to what to do with them next. You can:

- Arrange for them to be scattered in the grounds of the crematorium (by prior arrangement).

Most crematoria have a Garden of Remembrance where the loose ashes can be strewn. You can do this, by arrangement, when you pick up the ashes or you can wait until a few days have passed if you wish. This will normally be free of charge.

If you want a more permanent record of the cremation, there will be a Book of Remembrance in which, for a small fee, you can enter the deceased's name and details (see Chapter 8).

You may be able to bury the container in the grounds of the crematorium, or lodge it, marked by a plaque, in an area set aside for that purpose, but this is not a facility many crematoria can offer.

- Have them buried in the grounds of a local cemetery.

- You can purchase a burial site for ashes containers in exactly the same way as you can for a coffin (see Chapter 5), together with a marble or granite container and grave marker if desired.

**Ⓗ**  The comments in Chapter 5 about purchasing a burial site also apply here. Go and look around a crematorium or cemetery to see where the different grave sites are situated. One might appeal to you more than others: it is often hard to tell how things will strike you when all you have to go on is a brief description or a piece of paper.

- Arrange for the ashes to be buried in a churchyard.

- Take them home with you.

- Arrange for them to be transported to another location, either for storage there, or to be scattered, for example, at sea. Most crematoria will not arrange transportation for ashes, but if this is desired – perhaps the deceased wanted his remains to return to his place of birth in another part of the UK, or even in a different country – your funeral director can contact courier companies and make the arrangements for you.

## How do I know they are the deceased's ashes?

Crematoria have a very strict Code of Conduct and this covers the actual process of cremation. Each coffin has an identity card, and this travels with the coffin at each stage. There can be no mix-up as the cremator can only accept one coffin at a time.

## ❶ Make Sure You Know How Much it Will All Cost

This depends greatly on whether the coroner is involved or not (if he is, you won't have to pay the doctors' fees for signing the certificates) and the fees charged by the individual cemetery.

The doctors' fees for signing Forms B and C will cost a minimum of £34.50 each.

For the actual cremation, on average, you might expect to pay £150 plus (1996 prices), but because of wide regional variations, do not be surprised if you are charged more or less. Expect to pay more if the deceased did not live in the crematorium's catchment area.

You also will have to pay if you are going to have the ashes buried, either in the crematorium grounds if this is possible (which it often isn't), or in a cemetery. This will probably cost you £50 or more, again depending on the individual cemetery and the part of the country in which you live.

On top of this, if you want the ashes transported to that site rather than taking them yourself, you will have to arrange this with the crematorium and of course, there will be a fee.

What can be said with certainty is that the after-death costs are far less than where there is a full-sized grave to maintain. Even if you purchase a marble or granite container or grave marker for the ashes and a burial site, the overall costs of after-death care are lower.

# 7

# Arranging a Religious Ceremony

Most people are relatively untouched by death in the early part of their lives. The only deaths in the immediate family are likely to be those of their grandparents, and all the funeral arrangements are handled by their children – your parents. For some reason, the knowledge they gain of what to do when someone dies is rarely handed on. Perhaps it is felt that children and young adults should not be too closely involved in such matters. Perhaps, also, it is felt that there is no hurry to do so: after all, the people who have just done the organizing are too young to need the services of a funeral director themselves in the near future. Time goes by, and the knowledge and expertise is lost as the subject remains undiscussed. The result is that when you yourself have to bury parents, brothers, sisters, uncles, aunts or even, tragically, your own children, the whole business is something of a mystery, and you have to start the learning process from scratch.

The aim of this book is to give you the information you need at that stressful time, and the specific purpose of this chapter is to help you make the best use of the religious service which most people hold before the burial or cremation. The funeral service is the time when you can forget about all the practical tasks you have had to cope with, and focus on grief and mourning. Such a ceremony is a highly emotional experience, even for those not particularly close to the deceased.

The comments below apply to a Christian ceremony as Christians form the largest religious group in this country.

Even if you are a committed and practising Christian you may find the advice helpful as you may never have attended or organized a funeral service. The chapter is primarily aimed, though, at those born into the Christian faith who are not regular churchgoers and who may not know what to do or what to expect. It will help you to organize a service, and anticipate the moments that are likely to affect you the most. Please take any references to a church to mean any place in which a religious service is held, such as the Chapel of Rest at a crematorium.

**❶ Decide Whether You Want the Ceremony Held in a Church, the Crematorium Chapel or at the Graveside**

If you want a religious ceremony, you can opt to have it in the deceased's parish church, at the crematorium chapel if he is being cremated, or at the graveside. You need to tell the minister this, either in person or through the funeral director. If he has to travel to get there, he will need to allocate time for this.

**❶ Choose the Service**

This may be quite a daunting task if you are not a regular churchgoer. You are being asked to arrange something about which you have very little specific knowledge. You might be confronted with questions you cannot answer, such as 'What hymns do you want?' or 'What readings are you going to have?' What do you do?

- If these questions are being posed by other relatives and close friends, ask what their preference is. You might also ask if they know of any favourites the deceased might have had.

- Admit your ignorance to the minister of religion and ask him for suggestions. Don't be afraid to do so: quite a high proportion of Christians in this country are not regular churchgoers and might need such advice. He will be accustomed to helping in this way.

**❶**     If you have no idea which minister might take the service, ask your funeral director. He will know those who can be the most helpful to you in this situation.

### If the deceased wasn't a regular churchgoer

Just because the deceased might not have attended church regularly does not necessarily mean that he had rejected his religion. However, although this situation will leave you with no guidance to his preferences, you might feel that leaving the choice entirely to the minister makes the whole service somewhat impersonal. What is said and sung should, after all, have some specific connection with the deceased.

In these circumstances you might think of themes or principles which meant a lot to the deceased in his life. Perhaps he was a strong believer in peace, or was especially fond of children. Perhaps he was a highly honourable man, or one who had fought for his country. You could then discuss these with the minister to find texts and hymns which highlight these aspects of the deceased's life and beliefs.

### If the deceased attended church regularly

Here, your problem is much easier. If the deceased attended church regularly he will be known to the minister of religion and you can jointly work out what the deceased might have appreciated.

## 🅣 Be Honest with the Minister

Most ministers will be immensely sympathetic and helpful, and will welcome suggestions from you. It is possible, however, that you will come across one who appears to be a little less understanding. In all probability this will be because he has an abrupt manner rather than an uncaring attitude, but if you are unsure of your rights and needs, it might be tempting in these circumstances to let him take over totally, thus effectively excluding you from design of the ceremony.

Quite simply, don't allow this to happen. Be constructive, not confrontational (which will get you absolutely nowhere), and explain that you want his help in designing a service which celebrates the life of the deceased, and his beliefs and values. You are sorry that you are not able to offer concrete suggestions, but this is really very important to you and the other mourners.

## Elements of the Service which Can be Personalized

Personalizing a service is a task you can undertake with loving care even if you are out of touch with Christian practice.

### Hymns

If the deceased had favourite hymns, choose one or more of these – the last time they will be sung before his body is interred. If he did not, choose ones which are appropriate with the help of the minister. (Some suggestions are included in Appendix 2.)

🅗    If the words of the hymn are particularly important to you, pop into a church and skim through one of the hymn books to find the words that 'speak to you'.

🅗    Think whether it is wise to have hymns if only a few people are going to turn up. It will be bad enough if they all know the words to the hymns and the tune, but if they don't, who is going to sing them? If you still want music, ask the organist simply to play the melody.

Arranging a Religious Ceremony  69

## Address by the minister

The minister will speak a few words about the deceased. Clearly, if the minister knew him he can speak with confidence from personal knowledge. If he did not, it is up to you to supply the information. Tell the minister a little about his life – his triumphs and failures, his beliefs and values. Offer a few anecdotes. The minister might not use all this but it will help him form a good picture of the deceased and will enable him to say something that is appropriate and satisfying. There is nothing worse than hearing a minister make a bland statement about someone being a good and holy man, when everyone present knew he was sharp-tempered and tight-fisted. If in that situation, however, the minister had known more about the deceased he might have said – truthfully – that the deceased always made sure he could provide for his family and that he was quick to speak up against injustice. You and the other mourners then know the minister was talking about a real person, and not just 'the deceased'. Unless you provide this information, though, the minister cannot help you.

## Address by family or friends

Many churches allow an address by one or more family or friends. They can use this to talk briefly about the deceased and his life.

**H** If someone has volunteered to do this, advise him to jot a few notes on a piece of card and put it in his pocket. He will probably want to speak from the heart, but he can use this card if he freezes when the time comes.

## Texts

The book containing the order of service, which will be made available to you, contains a selection of texts (and hymns) which you can use if you wish, although you do not have to. If there is going to be a reading, why not make sure the words mean something to those listening? The words can have great value, even if some of the congregation are not practising Christians, or are of another faith. (Sample texts are given in Appendix 2.)

If you have the option of these texts being read by lay people, think carefully about whether you yourself could handle the task. You may want to do this as a labour of love: you should, however, be sure you are not going to break down completely. Don't forget that speaking in public is an ordeal for most people at the best of times. You can always ask for volunteers from among the deceased's friends and family, or decline this option altogether.

By personalizing a service you can design a public statement that this person lived, and the world was a better place because of it. When the funeral service actually takes place, it is extremely comforting to hear this. The deceased was loved and achieved at least some of the things he set out to achieve. Even if his final illness was painful, there were times of great happiness in his life. Take this opportunity to be glad that the deceased experienced those good times.

Once you have reached agreement on a service you think is right, you can feel the minister is speaking for you and for anyone else who cared. It becomes a public statement of your grief. You have a right to grieve, and an understanding minister should help you do so through the service.

**Ⓣ Write out/Print the Order of Service and Name of Hymns, and Duplicate It**

Even the regular churchgoers will find an order of service helpful. This task is usually done by the bereaved's family rather than the church.

**Ⓗ**     If you don't have a typewriter or word processor, write down the order of service and take it to a print shop. They will be able to have it typeset for you quickly and (relatively) cheaply.

**Ⓣ Understand What Moments Are Likely to Affect You**

Entering the church

Your first really bad moment, if the deceased is to be buried, is likely to be when you enter the church and see the coffin. That coffin, in full public view, contains someone you knew as a live and interesting human being. Now his remains are sealed inside a container, and this service is part of an inexorable process that will lead to those remains being buried or cremated. No matter how much you prepare for it, it is a shock. If the deceased is to be cremated and the service is being held at the crematorium chapel, you will probably walk in behind the coffin.

If you are one of the main mourners you will be seated at the front of the church, near the coffin. It is likely you will be painfully aware of it no matter where you try to look. You will quite possibly want to cry. The best advice is to let nature have its way: it is well known that open grieving after a death is part of the healing process. So if you want to cry, you probably need to, and should. The sight of the coffin might well trigger this off.

**H**   Stand near someone who knows when to stand up and sit down, if you are not used to attending religious ceremonies. You don't need to be worrying about that when you are mourning and possibly in tears.

## Hymns

Most people will opt for one or more hymns. This is a chance for you to regain your self control if you want to. You have something to focus on other than what lies ahead. If you know the hymns, sing them. If you don't, follow the words and try to sing the parts you can. Treat this as a respite.

## Readings

There may be readings from the Bible or other religious book, either by the minister or by family members or friends. The solemnity of the readings and the tone in which they are read can be upsetting, but try to listen to the words and gain comfort from them. If you have chosen them, the texts will carry special meaning. Focus on this meaning and how it relates to the deceased.

## Prayers

Join in if you can. If you have religious beliefs you know you are offering a prayer to someone who is listening. If you don't, well, can you absolutely guarantee that it is a wasted effort? If there is a chance that prayer will benefit the deceased, take it. The mere act of speaking the words will somewhat lessen your emotional pain.

## Address by the minister/family

This is another period that might distress you. The minister should say a few words from the pulpit specifically about the deceased whom he will name and say is now departed. It is a public statement that our loved one is dead, and this will emphasise the finality. Hearing the list of good things he did, and the fact that he was respected will make you remember, and make you aware that these times are gone, forever. Again, if you want to cry, do so.

Sometimes, however, you might be amused as old memories are revived. Do not feel you always have to cry at funerals: some people specifically ask for their funeral services to be a joyful celebration of their life. If you find yourself smiling or laughing, do not feel you are breaking a taboo.

## Removal of the coffin from church for burial

This is usually the most traumatic moment of the whole service. The coffin will be lifted by the bearers and carried from the church. You somehow have to find sufficient composure to get to your feet and follow it, knowing that the remains of your loved one are being taken out for disposal. You have also already sat through a service which will almost certainly have upset you considerably. This is the point at which most people break down. It is the final goodbye until the grave itself. Two suggestions might be helpful. The first is to give in to your grief. The second is to ensure, before the service, that you are sitting near someone perhaps slightly less emotionally involved who can physically help you if you become distressed. This is not a moment when you should try to cope on your own. Knowing this beforehand might help.

## Outside the church

There will be people in the congregation who will want to express their condolences. This might seem like the last thing you want to deal with at this time, but it is surprisingly comforting to hear one person after another say how much they valued the deceased and how much they will miss him. You don't need to make polite conversation, or indeed say anything at all – a brief thank you or a handshake will suffice.

## Going into the cemetery

Cemeteries are incredibly peaceful places. Make a conscious effort to be aware of this and use it to help you. Look around at the trees, the grass and the flowers and say to yourself that though, of course, you did not want the deceased to die, if he had to, this is a beautiful place in which to be laid to rest. You may see other families standing by an open grave. You are sharing something with them which cannot be put into words. You are not alone.

## The graveside

The sight of the open grave is usually devastating. Thoughts may come into your mind about what is to follow, not just immediately, but what will happen to the deceased's body over the coming weeks. Push these thoughts away. Tell yourself they are degrading to the deceased as an individual. You can be factual about what happens at a later stage. The lowering of the coffin is a terrible moment. Within seconds you know you must walk away and leave the deceased alone, truly dead and departed. There are two things you can do to try to lessen your pain – doing something, as a general principle, is always beneficial. The first is gently to throw a flower, or flowers, into the grave on top of the coffin. Choose flowers which meant something special to the deceased or to yourself. The second is to tell yourself very firmly that this is not a final goodbye, that you will return tomorrow, or the day after, and sit quietly by the grave to make sure the deceased is not alone. It lessens the break. It would be wrong to suggest you retreat from reality and pretend the death did not take place, but there is no reason to increase your agony by pretending the deceased will cease to exist. He – or at least his body – will be there for you to visit at a time when you don't have others around you, and you can say your goodbyes in privacy and at your own speed.

## The crematorium

The awfulness of the impending interment can be made worse if you don't know what to expect and let your imagination run away with you. In fact, the service will be like a service in a church, except that instead of a journey to the cemetery afterwards, the coffin will be hidden behind a screen or curtain at the end of the service and then borne away to the cremator. All the above comments about church services apply, but one thing that might catch you unawares is the speed with which the end comes. If you are not prepared for this it may be a wrenching shock. If at all possible, spend a few quiet moments with the coffin the night before the service – you don't need to see the deceased if you find it distressing, but it is comforting to say a quiet goodbye.

## In the grounds of the crematorium

You may want to spend a few minutes after the ceremony looking at the floral tributes which will have come to the crematorium with the coffin. It is also often helpful to wander around the grounds and the Garden of Remembrance. As with cemeteries, the grounds are often extremely tranquil places and might give you back some of your peace of mind.

**H**     Take some time to walk around the grounds. This might well be the only time you have to yourself during the entire day, especially if you are offering refreshments to mourners.

It would be foolish to pretend that funeral services are anything but an ordeal for those closest to the deceased, but they can also provide emotional comfort and reassurance. If you bear this in mind when you design the service, you and the other mourners can see it as a celebration of the deceased's life and achievements, as well as a statement that he is now dead.

# 8

# Upkeep of Graves

When you are arranging a funeral it is hard to think beyond the actual burial or cremation. You might, however, want to consider how the grave site is to be maintained and, planning ahead a little, whether you want to erect a headstone or memorial tablet as a tribute to the deceased. What exactly are your options and how much will it cost?

## Facts You Should Know

There is a range of services you can purchase to tend and beautify the grave after the burial has taken place, whether the deceased was buried in a coffin or his ashes were buried in a container. These fall into two basic categories:

- Maintenance contracts: turfing, weeding, etc.
- Headstones and memorial tablets.

Some local authority cemeteries offer a very complete range of these services while others offer only a few, but will permit you to make your own arrangements with stonemasons. Most churchyards will be limited in the services they can provide.

All of these options will be discussed below. However, for now you should know that while you can arrange for a maintenance contract for the grave site immediately after the burial, some time must elapse before you can erect a permanent headstone or memorial. This is to allow the ground to settle after having been disturbed. The actual length of time involved depends on the part of the country in which the burial took place: if the ground is sandy, you may looking at a period of six months before you can erect anything on the grave site, but where the ground is mainly clay you may be looking at as much as a year.

This time lapse, which may be frustrating on one hand, does give you time to think carefully about what you want and to commission an appropriate grave marker should you decide to do so.

## ⓣ Be Realistic

It might be useful at this point to give you a warning. In the emotion of the moment it is easy to decide on a magnificent headstone and every maintenance contract on offer, to ensure you provide the deceased with the best grave and tribute possible. Consider four things:

- Would the deceased himself have wanted you to spend money on these thing?

- Can you, or the deceased's estate, really afford it?

- How much satisfaction is it going to give you in relation to the money you will spend?

- Do you genuinely want to do this, or are you feeling somewhat pressured by people around you?

The decision as to how much to spend is, of course, up to each family. Some will feel unsatisfied unless they have provided the very best they can afford. Others will see this as a complete waste of money. It is your decision. All that is suggested here is that it is wise to step back and think about it before committing yourself; then if you decide to go ahead you can do so without regrets and recriminations cropping up when you come to write the cheque.

It goes without saying that it might be right for some people to let nature take its course with the grave, allowing it to gradually become covered with weeds and wild flowers. The only correct decision as to what to do about the grave once the deceased has been buried is the one that is right for those left behind.

## ⓣ Find Out What You Are Allowed To Do

Before you make any decisions, and certainly before you commission any headstone or memorial tablet, there is one thing you must do. You absolutely must find out what is and is not allowed by the cemetery or churchyard in which the deceased is buried. Some cemeteries permit only the simplest of tablets while others allow you a very wide choice indeed; some cemeteries only allow the most minimal of headstones, being maintained mostly as lawn. It is the same with wording. Some sites, particularly churchyards, can be very restrictive about the inscriptions that are permitted. Check this out before you set your heart on something and then find it is forbidden.

You should also ask if any special restrictions apply to public (non-exclusive) graves, if this affects you.

## Whom to approach

If the deceased is buried in a cemetery, speak to the cemetery manager or his staff, and if possible, get them to detail any restrictions in writing: it is so easy to forget or misunderstand what has been said in a telephone conversation, or a discussion in the cemetery office with phones ringing and people popping in and out. If the deceased is buried in a churchyard, talk to the vicar or priest.

## Burial – Options Available

Not all options are available at all cemeteries or churchyards, but among the things you might want to ask are:

- The cost of an annual maintenance agreement for the grave, and exactly what this covers.
- Whether there is a turfing service.
- Whether a temporary grave marker is allowed until the soil has settled.
- Whether headstones and memorials are permitted, and if so:
  – The maximum permitted size.
  – Any constraints on materials used.
  – Any constraints on design.
- Whether figurines are allowed.
- What the guidelines are for inscriptions.
- Whether foreign lettering is permitted.
- Whether there any constraints on colour in the stone, lettering or design used.
- Whether marble kerb surrounds are permitted.
- Whether photo plaques are allowed.
- The policy on markers for ashes containers.

All this is likely to be completely new to you so it might be useful to discuss some of them in detail.

Do not look round the cemetery or churchyard and assume that what has been permitted in the past will be permitted now.

## 🛈 Learn More About the Options You Have

### Maintenance contracts

You can often arrange for the grave to be cared for at regular intervals throughout the year. This might cover cutting the grass, weeding, ensuring that shrubs and creepers do not intrude on the grave, and generally doing what is necessary to keep the grave carefully tended. Some sites will offer all these services under the general heading of maintenance while others will offer basic cutting and weeding, and offer the other services separately.

Check how often the maintenance will take place – twice yearly, four times yearly, etc. Also check how long a period is covered by the maintenance fee you pay: in many places you will be expected to pay a fee annually to cover a one-year contract.

Note that few cemeteries are happy about you tending the grave yourself to any major extent; while they might turn a blind eye to your clipping the grass with a pair of scissors, they will not welcome the appearance of a mower or cans of weedkiller. Before committing yourself to a contract, find out exactly what, if anything, you will be allowed to do yourself.

## Availability of a turfing service

Turfing means the laying of a smooth grass surface across the top of the grave, instead of allowing grass to grow irregularly and interspersed with small weeds. Another option sometimes offered is banking and turfing. This means that the grave will be turfed, but earth will be piled on top of the grave beforehand to raise it above the level of the surrounding ground.

## Temporary grave markers

As explained above, you will almost certainly have to wait some time until the ground has settled before a permanent grave marker can be erected, and the length of time will depend on the type of soil in the area. In some places where the soil type dictates that the wait will be extensive, perhaps years, you are sometimes able to erect temporary markers above the grave. The cost of these will, of course, be considerably less than for a permanent marker.

## Headstones and memorials

To commission a gravestone or memorial you need to go to a stonemason. Despite the name, he usually works in other materials, such as marble, as well. If you have used a funeral director, he might have links with a mason and can recommend him.

If you look through a stonemason's brochure you will probably be surprised at the variety of shapes on offer.

**H**  Wander around the cemetery on a quiet afternoon and see what type of memorial attracts your eye.

You can obviously opt for a simple square tablet erected at the head of the grave as a marker, but nowadays you might be able to choose one shaped like a book to represent the Bible, or one with a design engraved into it. Even the simple cross can have variations: many people of Irish or Scottish origin opt for a Celtic cross to mark the grave of the deceased.

You are likely to find there is a maximum permitted size for any grave marker: it is extremely unlikely that it will be allowed to be larger than the grave and there will almost certainly be a maximum permitted height. The days of the extravagant Victorian memorials have passed.

You will want to choose a material which lasts and which can withstand the British climate over the years, so your choice is likely to be between marble, granite and stone. There is more than one type of each of these, indeed, the varieties available are surprising. Most people will opt for a grey or white colour, but it is possible to have coloured, or colour-flecked versions of some materials.

## Figurines

Figurines are little statues of, for example, angels or doves. They stand separately–that is, they are not carved into the actual stone or marble – but are secured on the grave marker or on the memorial. Again, some places will permit these and some will not.

## Inscriptions

You will almost certainly find that there are restrictions on the wording you can use, though some places are more liberal than others about what is allowed: other places, especially some churchyards, have restrictions that might surprise you. You will also find that there is a maximum number of permitted words.

A couple of examples will illustrate the kind of thing you should think about:

- You might find the word 'Mother' perfectly acceptable, but use of the word 'Mum' forbidden, even though 'Mum' was how she was known in life. There are some sites which have a policy of forbidding short forms of names – 'William' would be allowed but 'Bill' would not, and very few places are keen on nicknames.

- The other thing you should ask about is the policy on dates. Some sites insist on the dates in numbers – 'Died 11.2.94', while others prefer some or all of the date spelt out – 'Died 11 February 1994'. You may find that some sites will allow both the birth and death dates while others will only accept the date of death to be inscribed on the grave marker.

**H**   Look around a cemetery and see what other inscriptions have been used.

Some of the favourite inscriptions are shown in Appendix 3.

## Foreign lettering

This is quite an important issue for certain ethnic groups within this country. One example of this might be of someone born in Poland who fled here during the communist years, eventually making his home and dying here. His name will probably have contained all kinds of characters which are not in the English alphabet. His family might well ask why his grave should bear a name which was not his, that is, the anglicized version, leaving out the correct Polish letters. Some cemeteries, particularly those in multicultural areas, have met this problem enough times now to permit foreign lettering on graves.

You may, on the other hand, find if you ask about this that this is the first time the managers of the site have had to consider the matter. If they say it is not allowed, it is always worth asking whether this is a specific policy, that is, the matter has been actively considered because of past requests.

## Coloured materials, lettering or design

As explained above, some of the materials used to make headstones and memorials come in different colours, or have coloured flecks. Of these, probably the most dramatic is polished black granite, often engraved with a design. Some cemeteries and churchyards allow the use of these while others do not.

Because of techniques in masonry not available to earlier generations, it is now possible to have coloured designs sandblasted into the material chosen for the headstone or memorial. These might be angels, a spray of roses, or even something to indicate the deceased's hobby or occupation. These can look extremely effective and are permitted in cemeteries with a liberal policy towards grave markers, but if you think the idea attractive, you should check this before going ahead with the commission.

## Kerb surrounds

You may not know the term but you would recognize marble or granite kerb surrounds if you saw them. This is where the whole area over the top of the grave is covered in marble chips, and these are surrounded on all four sides by a small wall of marble a couple of inches high. Sometimes the wall is thick enough to contain a small depression in which a vase of flowers can be placed. This can look very attractive, especially when the marble chips are coloured.

### Photo plaques

This is an idea which you will often see in cemeteries in certain parts of Europe and which is becoming increasingly popular over here.

A small photograph of the deceased is reproduced, placed under glass, mounted in a metal frame and inserted into the grave marker. Thus, not only does the grave bear his name but anyone passing by, and friends and relatives visiting the grave, have a constant reminder of what the person buried there actually looked like in life. Many people believe this helps to keep the memory of the person alive and doesn't reduce him to a name and a date.

**(H)**   When choosing a photo, think whether you want to remember the deceased as he was when he died, or, if he was elderly, you would rather have a picture of him when he was younger. Don't forget that old photos can nowadays be retouched, using computer and other techniques.

### Markers for ashes containers

These will, of course, be smaller than markers for graves. You may find the designs permitted need to be simpler than those possible for graves and, of course, there is less surface area on which to inscribe wording. However, if the cemetery has a liberal policy, some of the possibilities discussed above might be of interest to you in designing the marker.

## **(T)** Cost It All Out Carefully

Don't forget to add in all the little extras – these can add up surprisingly fast.

### Upkeep of memorials

Stone, marble and granite are strong materials but they will not last forever. Over the years they will be eroded by wind and rain, cracks may form and the edges may crumble.

You can arrange to have these memorials cleaned on a regular basis and inspected for damage which can be repaired either by the site managers or by a stonemason hired by you.

If you have a second person interred in that grave, the grave marker will have to be removed first and then replaced. Inevitably, this may result in damage, not because of carelessness on anybody's part but because the material might have become weakened. If you do have a second interment, be aware of this possibility and account for it in your estimation of costs.

## Purchase of memorials and tablets

It is impossible to quote average figures as these will vary enormously from place to place, subject to the availability of material – one material which might be scarce in one part of the country, and thus very expensive, might be cheap in another.

In general one can say that the most expensive grave markers are likely to be the marble or granite kerb surrounds, while at the other end of the scale you should be able to purchase a modest headstone for under £400, and possibly well below that price in some areas. Do not abandon the idea if £400 seems a lot of money – this is just offered as a reasonable average price for a small grave marker: you may well find something a great deal cheaper by phoning around. You may also have to pay for a permit allowing you to erect the grave marker.

## Maintenance and removal of memorials and tablets

Maintenance of memorials is not as expensive as you might expect and in most cases will be well under £100 per year. In some parts of the country it might be a fraction of this figure.

Removal and replacement is more expensive but if you estimate £100 you will not be far wrong – it may be a little more, it may be a little less, but that gives you a rough idea of what to expect.

**H**  Ask if there are any permit fees for erecting headstones: these can suddenly appear as hidden costs after you have commissioned the work from the mason.

## Cremation – the Options Available

Where a cremation has taken place, the relatives need to decide whether to:

- Bury the ashes in a container, either in the crematorium grounds if this is allowed, or elsewhere.
- Have the ashes scattered (see pages 63-4).

- Retain the ashes, eg at home (see page 64).

## A Tribute to the Deceased

Whether the ashes are buried or scattered, there are a number of ways in which the deceased's death can be marked. Not all cemeteries and crematoria will offer all of these, but the most common options you will be able to purchase are:

- An entry in a Book of Remembrance.

- A wall or ground plaque.

- A grave marker: either a vase, container or tablet.

- A rosebush, shrub or tree with an inscribed plaque.

- A donated item such as a bench or a stained-glass window in the deceased's name for use in the crematorium or cemetery grounds or in the chapel.

The warning, as always, is that you may not be offered all these options. You will have to pay for them, and many of these options will be offered for fixed periods, after which you will have to renew the agreement and pay a further fee.

### Entry in the Book of Remembrance

Each crematorium will keep an official book in which you can enter the deceased's details.

You may be limited to a standard entry of, say, one or two lines or you may have the option of purchasing a longer entry allowing you to provide more details of the deceased, or perhaps to add a phrase such as 'Gone but never forgotten'.

You might also, in some places, be allowed to add a coat of arms or a service badge after the name, or even a small design.

The Book of Remembrance will be displayed in a special area of the crematorium and usually the entries for a particular date will be displayed on that date.

An entry in the Book of Remembrance involves a fixed fee: once you have paid this you will not be required to pay any further money.

### Purchase of a wall or ground plaque

A plaque is simply another word for a small square or rectangular piece of material on which an inscription is written.

The material often used is either marble or granite, though some cemeteries and crematoria will allow leather, or even perspex. You will be allowed up to a set number of words for your inscription (the comments on inscriptions on pages 78-9 also apply here), and this plaque will be hung on one of the crematorium's walls or set into the ground, usually for an agreed period of time. If you want the plaque to remain on display for longer than this you will have to renew the agreement.

## A grave marker

These can take many forms, although you must check what the maximum permitted size is and ask if there are any restrictions on what is allowed (see page 78).

If you intend to bury the ashes and want an elegant container, a stonemason will be able to offer you a range of shapes made out of a number of different materials. These might be square, rectangular, or shaped more like a traditional vase.

They can be quite simple or can have a design such as an angel or a dove of peace etched into or sandblasted on to them.

You might also want to buy a flat tablet on which to place this; thus if, for example, you have chosen a square container of polished black granite, you might want to rest this on a flat slab of the same material. You can often buy the two separately or you can choose a design which incorporates the two.

Some people like to add a small figurine to 'guard' the grave site. This is often an angel or some other figure which implies hope or peace.

## Rosebush, shrub or tree

Some people like the idea of having a tribute to the deceased which will grow and give pleasure over the years. Many, though not all, cemeteries allow the planting of a rosebush, shrub or even a tree above the grave site. These will come with a small inscribed plaque. Do note, however, that you must approach the site managers, make your selection, pay the correct fee and then leave the planting to them: you cannot turn up at the grave site with a rosebush under one arm, a spade under the other, and start digging!

Whether this is a one-off payment with the plaque remaining in perpetuity or whether it is for a fixed term of years depends very much on the individual burial site, but in most places you will pay for a specific number of years. If you want the plaque to remain in place below the shrub or rosebush, you must renew the contract. Some places, however, will allow you, for a larger sum, to purchase the planting of a tree and this tree remains permanently dedicated to the deceased.

## Donation of an item

If you can afford it, this is an excellent way to commemorate the deceased as it will give pleasure to a number of people – perhaps themselves grieving – who pass through the crematorium or cemetery. Typical donations might be a bench, with a small metal plaque fixed to the back inscribed with the name of the deceased, or a small stained-glass window for the chapel.

If this idea attracts you, always check first with the site managers before committing yourself, but such gifts are invariably very welcome. Especially in sites run by local authorities there is usually only limited money to spend on such things, but there is no doubt that they make a great deal of difference to the appearance and facilities of the area.

## 🛈 Cost It All Out Carefully

### Upkeep of memorials

All the comments relating to the upkeep of memorials over graves apply here. You may want to arrange for the container or grave marker to be cleaned at regular intervals and any damage repaired. You may also want to be notified when your fixed term of years for a rosebush and plaque runs out. You should ask the cost of these when you apply.

In general, the cost of a grave marker, container or tablet where ashes are buried as opposed to a coffin is much lower; indeed, you may find you can purchase a container for below £100 in some places.

A simple entry in the Book of Remembrance might cost below £50, with additional costs for more lines. A plaque will depend on the material from which it is made, but again should cost around £100.

### Memorials for a Child

If the deceased is a child, you might find it far more appropriate to have a memorial designed especially for a child. Some stonemasons offer this service and cemeteries are often quite understanding about what it permitted in these circumstances. You might, for example, want a teddy bear engraved on the headstone. (See also Chapter 18.) or you might also want an inscription more appropriate to a child. (See Appendix 3.)

# Part II

# *People and Possessions*

# 9

# Dealing with Family and Friends

There are a great number of people you are going to have to tell about the death over the next few weeks. Some of these will have to be notified almost as soon as the death has occurred, and these are family and friends of the deceased. In practical terms this means you will have to deal with a number of people, many of whom you might not know personally, each claiming a differing degree of closeness to the deceased, which may or may not be true. Hopefully, things will go smoothly but there is the potential for trouble. This chapter focuses on how to handle these people before, and particularly at and after, the funeral.

## ❶ Contact Relatives and Close Friends

As far as possible, anyone who was close to the deceased should be contacted before the funeral. They will want to hear the news, and you should give them the chance to express their grief no matter how deep your own distress.

Do not feel frustrated or that you have let the deceased down if there are people you cannot trace: you can only do your best and you are not psychic.

You may have to contact friends and relatives of the deceased that you don't know personally. See how they respond to the news. If they obviously cared, remember this. If they come to the funeral you might want to make a special effort to speak to them: if not, you might want to phone or write to them later.

## ❶ Be Firm If You Only Want a Small Funeral

If you have decided on a small funeral, explain this and most people will not wish to intrude. If that is your decision, stick to it. If someone insists on coming after you have made this clear, they are being extremely insensitive and you need to be polite but firm. Say simply that you really appreciate the fact that they wish to be there but you are very sorry – it is a family decision to restrict the numbers.

**⊕** Blame the decision on 'the family'. The awkward person can and probably will argue with you, because you are the person on the end of the phone or whose name they have. As you will know if you've tried to argue with a government or local authority department, it is far harder to argue if you are not quite sure exactly who has actually made the decision that has upset you.

There may be sound reasons for your not wanting that person there. Some people, no matter how close to the deceased by blood, can grate on your nerves or cause trouble. Don't be emotionally blackmailed into inviting people to the funeral for form's sake.

**⊕** Tell them the date for the funeral has not yet been finalized. Lie if you have to.

**❶ Accept That You Will Not Feel Like Polite Conversation at the Funeral**

In most cases, unless you are having a very small funeral, it will be virtually impossible for you to get to know all the people who turn up for the service. Even if you knew the deceased's friends and contacts well, you are not going to feel much like conversation. Don't try to be sociable unless you want to. Most people will, if they approach you at all, simply shake your hand or give you a quick kiss and tell you how sorry they are. They will not expect more than a brief acknowledgement.

If someone is insensitive enough to try to start a longer conversation, you can excuse yourself politely and easily by saying that you have to speak to the vicar/funeral director/Aunty Maud, etc.

**❶ Decide Whether You Want to Offer Refreshments After the Funeral**

This is often a good way of accepting condolences which you couldn't face at the church, crematorium or graveside. By offering refreshments you are showing you are not shutting these people out of your grieving: that it is something you are all going through.

If the idea appeals but you are not sure you can cope, be honest about this beforehand and enlist the help of a friend. If someone announces on your behalf that you are too upset to appear at the moment, everyone will understand. In that way, you achieve your objective – offering the hand of friendship to those close to the deceased – without having to cope with emotional comments which you might find too much at that time.

## ① Decide Whether to Offer Close Mourners a Memento of the Deceased

This usually takes the form of a small personal item of little monetary value.

Before you do this, be sure of the legal situation. If you are the surviving spouse, all the deceased's possessions are now yours and you can do what you want with them. However, if you are not, someone will inherit them and it may not be you. In that case, of course, you have no right to give the deceased's possessions away at all. Even if you have read the will and are sure you are the one to inherit, you really should do nothing for the moment. In most cases, probate has to be obtained and the estate valued (Chapters 14 and 16) before anyone can start disposing of the deceased's possessions.

In reality, of course, the immediate family may agree among themselves, and with the executor (see Chapter 14) that small items of little or no monetary value can be given as mementoes. This is often very much appreciated by those close to the deceased.

There are basically two ways to approach the selection of mementoes:

- You can select the mementoes yourself, choosing those that are appropriate to each individual; or

- You can ask the person involved to select something. The latter option is dependent on their sense and good taste.

### Selecting the mementoes yourself

If you opt to select the mementoes, you need to have some knowledge of the individuals concerned and their relationship to the deceased. Items you might like to consider are photographs, small items of clothing such as headscarves or gloves, low-value items relating to the deceased's work or personal interest, such as a small calculator or one of their own paintings (assuming it is of low monetary value), and favourite books. What you cannot give away (unless you are the surviving spouse) are items which will reduce the value of the estate, and which have a meaningful resale price.

In most cases this is not a problem. Genuine mourners are highly appreciative of any item belonging to the deceased which they can keep in their memory.

## Allowing mourners to choose mementoes

On the surface, this sounds more generous and more personal: each person can select something which has a meaning to them. You can explain to them that they should choose a small item. However, you are relying on them to keep to the rules you have laid down, and some people might not do this: there is nothing like the possible acquisition of something for nothing to bring out the worst in certain individuals. You may imagine someone is in the front room selecting the deceased's favourite book on train-spotting: it can be a nasty shock when they walk past you carrying that valuable crystal vase which has been in the family for generations. Getting them to part with it may be embarrassing and, sometimes, difficult.

In that situation you can:

- Quote the law at them. Say that nothing of any value at all can be given away until the estate is settled. This isn't always the case, especially if you are a surviving spouse, but they may not know this. If they do, simply shrug and say you yourself know nothing about the law: you are only obeying your solicitor. If they still persist, mutter about a special situation and grab the item. Few people, however greedy, will want a public scuffle at a funeral.

- Say that the item in question has special sentimental value to you, and you are sure they wouldn't have taken it if they had known.

One other option is to ask them to choose from a wide selection you have already made.

You can do this tactfully without spelling it out that you are restricting their options. You can simply say that you haven't had time to go through the deceased's effects thoroughly but you knew they would wish to have something belonging to the deceased and you have at least managed to find some items which you are sure the deceased would be delighted for them have as a memento. It is gentle, it is tactful and it enables you to keep control of the situation. Make sure these items are in one place so that there is no excuse for people to wander and pick up other things to which they are not entitled.

This sounds almost paranoid, and in most cases the problems will simply not occur. The sad truth, though, is that they happen often enough to be worth a mention.

## Ⓣ Be Prepared For Potential Tension Over the Will

Unfortunately, funerals – and the money and goods left by the deceased – bring out the worst in some people. Some of the most ferocious and long-lasting family squabbles start at the funeral with arguments over who has inherited what in the will. The most surprising people react in an avaricious manner, even those you would suppose are too deep in grief to think of such things.

This type of behaviour can manifest itself in a number of ways. If you have yet to make the terms of the will public, you might find condolences followed in the next sentence by a gentle but determined quizzing as to what the deceased left and to whom. You might be the target of pointed comments about your improved financial situation, or that of other members of the family. What do you do in these circumstances?

You pretend to ignore it. This is not the time to get into any kind of acrimonious discussion about money. If someone persists, say you are far too upset to think about such things at the moment, and walk away. If they have a right to know what is in the will, arrange to speak to them at a specific time in the near future.

## Ⓣ Responding to Alleged Promises of Possessions

If someone approaches you and tells you the deceased made him a personal promise that he should have a certain item, the thing to remember is that you do nothing for the moment. If it is the day of the funeral, say you know nothing about it and really can't consider it at that time. On the day of the funeral, that is almost unanswerable. Do not bow to emotional pressure and agree on the spot to hand it over. You need time to consider. Is it possible that a genuine promise was made? Does the item indeed have a particular meaning for the mourner? If so, the situation will not change if you give yourself a couple of days to consider.

Moreover, you can tell a great deal from the response of the mourner. A genuine mourner will not press the point. If he is angry and threatening, or attempts to use emotional blackmail, it is reasonable to suspect the sentimental value of the item means less to him than its monetary value. In all cases, ask for more details. When, exactly, was the promise made and were there any witnesses? Why is that particular item so important that nothing else will do?

In the end you will have to rely on your own judgement but listen to your instincts. You are under absolutely no obligation to give mementoes. If someone suggests he has a right to an item, put the onus of proving it on him. And bear in mind that unless you have inherited the entire estate, it will have to be valued. You cannot give away items of worth. Somehow it seems these situations never arise where the item has no monetary value at all.

## ❶ Resolve Not to Start a Feud

Don't forget that some people may act totally out of character because of the emotional trauma of the death. If bitter words are spoken, try to handle things gently, in a non-confrontational way – no matter how surprised or disgusted you feel. In this way you will not permanently alienate the person or start a family feud. If you handle things gently you are all free to pretend the incident never took place. If, after time has passed, you really feel you cannot forget the incident, you can allow the relationship quietly to lapse.

## ❶ Resolve Not to Have People Around If You Don't Want Them

Some people find that after the funeral they are suddenly terribly alone. Others find they are almost running a hotel and do not have the time or privacy to grieve.

This might be due to good intentions mixed with insensitivity on the part of family and friends, but remember that there are some people who need to feel needed, or at the centre of things, and are always there offering unwanted help when something goes wrong. It may sound harsh but that is their problem: you have enough of your own. If you don't want them around you must tell them to leave.

This can be easier said than done, as such people can be extremely persistent. If you have to, rely on lies and don't feel ashamed of this. Tell them you are visiting a friend or relative, and are leaving immediately. If they know you are isolated, tell them the doctor has advised you have no visitors. If you have to, speak to your local minister of religion or a friend and ask them to intervene. The important thing is that you gain the space you need to deal with the horrible reality of the death.

There is no doubt that friends and relatives can be an immense help and support in the days after a death. It is equally true that some of them can be a thorough menace, though sometimes with the best of intentions. Remember that as long as you have done your best to be polite to them and done what is proper in the circumstances, you have nothing to reproach yourself with if you fend off unwanted invitations. This is the time when people who care will take the trouble to find out what *you* want and need. Anyone who does anything else is not a friend, and should be kept at arm's length until you feel you can cope.

# 10

# People to Tell

It is tempting to believe that once the funeral has been arranged and the will sorted out that the hardest tasks are behind you. This is usually wishful thinking.

By this stage the number of people who know the deceased is in fact dead has started to grow. This number is likely to include the executor (if this is someone other than yourself), the Registrar, the funeral director, some family and friends. Depending on the circumstances of the death, it might also include the coroner and the local hospital. However, many other people with whom the deceased was in contact will still be in a state of ignorance. They will proceed on the basis that he will keep the appointment at the dentist, will turn up at the pub as usual on Thursday night, or will still be liable for Council Tax. They are not going to know any different unless somebody tells them. This someone is likely to be you, or someone close to you. In this chapter we are going to consider whom to tell, and how to tell them.

For all but the most isolated loners there are a surprising number of people who need to be notified within a relatively short time of a death. Some of these people will be known to those handling the deceased's estate: others will not. Identifying these people is a mixture of common sense and detective work. Unfortunately, it almost inevitably means going through the deceased's papers and personal possessions. This is an unpleasant task and you will probably feel you are invading his privacy. Don't worry – this is a common reaction. However, it is a duty you cannot avoid. What you can do is to carry it out with respect, dignity and efficiency. This chapter will help you to do so.

❶ Decide Who is to Contact Those Who Need to Know About the Death

This task is usually split between the family and the executor or administrator (see Chapter 14). The executor or administrator has a duty to contact people who need to know because money or property is involved, or because they are an official organization (like, for example, the Inland Revenue). The relatives generally handle breaking the news to personal contacts of the deceased.

## Ⓣ Tackle All the Deceased's Papers and Official Documents

Most people's passage through life is recorded on paper, for example, on credit cards, bills and as entries in an address book. Some people are tidy and file everything away neatly: many do not. The trick is to bring a sea of paper under control. The task is to separate the important pieces of information from those that are irrelevant, and to gather together information on particular subject areas.

Ⓗ      Go out and buy a dozen A4 envelope files, a black felt-tipped pen and some Post-Its (notelets with an adhesive strip on the back). Write on the front of each of the envelope files the category of papers you want to put inside, for example, 'Car', 'Utilities', 'Credit Cards'. As you go through the deceased's belongings, every time you find a piece of paper you think might contain useful information, put it straight into the relevant file. You may need to buy more files as you progress.

Useful file names might be:

- Medical.
- Friends and Relations.
- Gas/Electricity/Water Bills.
- Personal Finance, eg bank accounts and statements.
- Mortgage/rent.
- Local authority (eg Council Tax).
- Money from the state (eg pension).
- Credit cards.
- Car.
- Insurance policies.
- Death Certificates, etc.
- Employment.

If you can afford it, it might be a good idea to buy two more files, one labelled 'Souvenirs' for old letters, photos etc, and one labelled 'Miscellaneous', for those papers which look important but which completely mystify you. At the end of this task you will have brought a potentially unmanageable situation under control.

Every piece of paper you find should go into one of these files. Suddenly, a sea of papers has been reduced to a mere handful on any particular subject.

Ⓗ Don't act on the information immediately you find it: you may come across another piece of paper which makes your action unnecessary. Wait until you have been through all the papers and you are sure that all the details concerning, for example, 'Car' are together in one file.

After you have filed all the deceased's papers you will either have a complete picture and know exactly how to act, or know what is missing. Dealing with missing documents and information is dealt with in more detail in Chapter 11.

Ⓗ Label one of your A4 envelopes 'Friends and Relations'. This file is the exception to the rule of doing nothing until you have the whole picture, as friends and relations will need to be contacted straight away. If you are doing this before the funeral they may want to attend and need to arrange babysitters or take time off work. If you are doing it after the funeral they might feel upset and slighted if you do not tell them at the first opportunity. Perhaps this is unreasonable, but who is reasonable when they have lost someone they care about?

Ⓗ Phone or write to each friend or relation at the first opportunity. When you have done this, write 'Done' or something similar on the piece of paper or next to the name in the address book. This way, it becomes a task you can pick up and put down as you can always check exactly what you have and haven't done. To save you having to spend valuable time trying to find the right words, sample letters are included in Appendix 4. There are also suggestions as to the way in which you might break the news over the phone, as this is arguably more difficult: it is hard to think of the right thing to say when you are tense and upset yourself.

## ❶ Sort Out the Papers

When your filing is complete, sit down with your A4 envelopes, your Post-Its, a piece of blank paper and the list given on pages 98-9. Go down the list and check to see whether the relevant information is in the files. For example, the word 'Dentist' on the list should send you looking for the name and address of the deceased's dentist in your papers (perhaps in a file marked 'Medical'). Tick the list when you find the relevant information. At the end of this task you will have a clear picture of exactly what information is, and is not, available to you.

**Ⓗ**     On a separate piece of paper write down all the missing pieces of information. Discuss with others close to the deceased whether there is any valid reason for this information being missing: a ninety-year-old pensioner is, for example, unlikely to use an aromatherapist. If the absence of information is unreasonable you must turn detective. Chapter 11 will explain how to do this.

**Ⓗ**     As you handle each piece of paper, write the action you need to take on a Post-It, for example, 'Inform of death and send cheque for £3.68', and stick it on firmly. Make sure the ones that need urgent attention are on the top.

You will now know exactly which people and organizations you have to contact and what you need to do, but do have a look at the checklist overleaf if you get stuck.

## List of Contacts

### Accommodation
Mortgage deeds
Rent book
Tenancy agreement                    *private; council*

### Benefits
State pension book
DHSS                                 *Housing Benefit;*
                                     *Income Support;*
                                     *Invalidity Benefit;*
                                     *Girocheques;*
                                     *Child Benefit Book;*
                                     *Attendance Allowance;*
                                     *Mobility Allowance;*
                                     *National Insurance*

### Employer
Papers about pensions

### Financial
Insurance                            *life; medical; house and contents;*
                                     *valuable items*

Banks
Building societies
Post Office
Credit card companies

### Health Club/Gym

### Medical
Doctor                               *GP; specialist(s) at local hospital*
Dentist
Chiropodist
Osteopath
NHS Medical card

### Organizations
Membership cards                     *trade unions or associations; clubs;*
                                     *political organizations;*
                                     *subscriptions;*
                                     *volunteer co-ordinator*

### Pets
Name/address of vet
Pedigree certificates
Vaccination certificates

## Religion

Local church/synagogue/mosque/temple
Associated groups

## Social Services

Meals on wheels
Home help
Day care centre
Social worker

## State

Birth
Marriage
Death
Baptism
Adoption
Divorce
Immigration
Naturalization
Citizenship
Passport
Visas
Taxation
Council tax

## Transport

Car (motorbike, cycle etc)   *insurance; tax; MOT; credit arrangements; repairs and accident history; driving licence; registration documents/ ownership papers*

## Travel

Season ticket   *rail; bus*
OAP travel pass
Airline tickets

## Utilities

Water bill
Gas bill
Electricity bill
Telephone bill

It is worth looking at some of these in more detail.

## Accommodation

There are two crucial things to remember – notify the landlord or organization which holds the mortgage, and stay within the law. Neither of these should present a problem in normal circumstances and, in most cases, the disposal of the property runs smoothly. It is, possible, however, that a bad relationship existed between the deceased and the landlord, bank or building society, for example, where the mortgage was in arrears or where the landlord refused to undertake repairs. In these circumstances try not to be drawn into a dispute which is now effectively over. The building society may have been unreasonable. The landlord may have been a shark. All you want to do is to settle the matter as quickly as possible. If the disagreement affects the remaining family, explain that they are now dealing with someone different and try to negotiate with them. Be businesslike and detached in your dealings: what you say about them in the privacy of your own home is your own business!

This applies particularly when you feel the estate is at risk, for example, where there is a dispute over ownership. In these circumstances you will need to be able to think clearly. The last thing you need is a shouting match over the phone or a confrontation on the doorstep. If you feel there might be a serious problem, go and see a solicitor as quickly as possible. Remember three things. First, all reasonable legal costs will be paid by the estate, not by you personally. Second, the estate has legal rights, in the same way that a person does. The executor can act for the deceased even though he is no longer there to act for himself. Third, a solicitor can act as a negotiator in a tricky situation, thereby saving you a great deal of time and stress. The rule of thumb is, therefore – when in doubt, get legal advice. It may save you great deal of trouble in the long term.

## Benefits

If you have already registered the death with the Registrar (see Chapter 3) you will have received a form to send to Social Security. This should be enough to notify them that certain benefits are to be stopped and others paid to the executors of the estate. Anyone who lives in a large town or city knows, however, that it can take a considerable time for one department to notify another of any change in circumstances. In addition, you may need to start contacting people before registration of the death is possible, for example, where the coroner becomes involved. In this situation it is wise to write to the main departments individually, giving the deceased's claim number, particularly where the deceased was claiming a number of different benefits.

All benefit books should be returned to the DSS or handed in to the Post Office. If you are sending them by post, it is wise to send them recorded delivery. If you are handing them in at a Post Office, make sure you are given a receipt.

## Employer

Where the deceased had a contract of employment there should be few difficulties about receiving any pay due to the deceased up to the date of his death. Problems can occur where the deceased worked on a casual basis. It is easy to imagine a situation where an unscrupulous employer insists that the deceased was absent from work for the week prior to his death and that no money will be forthcoming for that period. This puts the onus on you to prove otherwise, which might be hard to do. The most important thing is to make it clear that you have no intention of giving up or being frightened away. The threat of legal action or a solicitor's letter often induces a sudden change of heart. At the end of the day, however, you must decide on the likelihood of success and balance this against the amount of money involved and the effort needed to extract this money. Because the executor has a legal duty to try to recover the money (see Chapter 14) visible efforts to reclaim it must be made. How far you pursue the issue is a matter of judgement in individual circumstances.

## Financial

When you are going through the deceased's papers trying to identify where his bank accounts are held, don't forget that there are a number of banks in addition to the Big Four – Lloyds, Midland, Barclays and National Westmister. If, for example, the deceased was Scottish, is it possible that would have an account with the Bank of Scotland or the Royal Bank of Scotland? If you feel this is likely but can find no evidence, note this is one area in which to carry out detective work (see Chapter 11).

The same principle applies to building societies. Many chains of building societies have a national presence but some do not, operating only in one particular region. If, for example, the deceased has recently moved from Bristol to London, is it possible that he would have retained an account in a building society such as the Bristol and West? If you think this is possible, put it on your list of things to check.

Insurance policies may present an even greater problem. Policies can be lost, or lodged in some as yet unidentified place. Payment books can be missing or duplicated (these matters are discussed in greater detail in Chapter 17). A complete absence of information on insurance policies should set the alarm bells ringing unless you have reason to believe the deceased was unlikely to have taken any out. Their existence or otherwise is important as money due under them counts towards the total value of the estate. A good place to start asking questions is the bank: they are likely to have asked the deceased whether he had insurance in order to assess his credit-worthiness.

## Health Club/Gym

It sounds mercenary but if the deceased held membership to a health club or gym (or indeed any other club), don't forget to ask whether a rebate of the unexpired portion of the membership can be given.

## Medical

The GP will usually have been contacted by this stage, either because the death occurred at home or by the hospital in order to help ascertain the cause of death. If you have reason to believe this has not been done, phone the surgery as soon as possible.

It is worth considering whether the deceased was visiting a specialist, such as a psychiatrist, or as a private patient in consulting rooms away from the hospital. In such a case there are likely to be letters confirming appointments and/or bills. As a commonsense rule of thumb the lower the deceased's income, the less likely this is to be the case.

Don't forget that many people these days visit alternative medicine practitioners, such as acupuncturists, chiropractors, Chinese herbalists and reflexologists, or attend holistic healing centres. Hopefully, you will find their details among the deceased's papers. However, appointments are often arranged by phone with the bill being paid on the day of the consultation, making written evidence hard to find (see Chapter 11 for details on how to track down these people).

Some alternative therapies have considerably more credibility than others. You may feel a lack of sympathy with some of the treatments, especially those on the fringes of alternative medicine. You may, indeed, feel that some of these people are charlatans and have been obtaining money by false pretences. There are two things to remember. Firstly, the deceased's life should be wound up with dignity and respect, and his outstanding debts must be paid. All that matters is that he believed the treatments would do him good. If he was willing to spend the money on alternative therapies while he was alive, what right do you have to go against his wishes now? Secondly, if the deceased was treated and there is an unpaid bill, it is a legal debt and must be paid out of the estate.

## Organizations

Try to reclaim the unexpired portion of any membership subscriptions. In searching for these, give thought to the deceased's interests – was he a supporter of any political party? What did the deceased do for a living – was it likely that he was a member of a trade or professional association? Also consider voluntary work. Did he have a particular interest in charity work, and if so, which charity was this likely to be? You might find indirect evidence of involvement, for example, half a dozen Greenpeace leaflets. One leaflet can be obtained in the street, half a dozen suggests a greater interest. A letter or a phone call will sort this out. If this seems unimportant, don't forget that someone may be counting on the deceased to play a part in a fund-raising event or to present a report.

There is another potential problem concerning charities which you should consider as you go through the deceased's effects – the question of donations. It may be that the deceased made regular donations to one or more charities. Details of these need to be noted. The executor or another member of the family may decide to continue these in memory of the deceased. Record the name of the charity now, before you lose the information.

## Pets

If there is a pet this is likely to be one of the problems you face unless the deceased has a surviving partner. Be aware that it is illegal to leave an animal on its own for extended periods: this is considered to be cruelty and a number of prosecutions have recently been brought on this basis.

The easiest thing to do is to leave the pet where it is, especially as it is likely to be distressed, and ask neighbours or friends to help. Offer them any reasonable inducement to do so. Don't forget that all essential expenses are borne by the estate. Looking after the pet is more than an essential expense – it is a legal obligation.

If this is not possible, you must arrange for the pet to be fostered out or to go to kennels, a cattery or similar. The Yellow Pages are a useful source of information in these circumstances. You might also ask the local vet for help. It is worth noting that boarding kennels or catteries will only take animals with certain vaccination certificates. If these cannot be found, your only options are either to pay or persuade someone to come in daily and feed it, or foster it. The best hope in either case is to contact a local animal charity. Many of these are very small – often only a handful of local people – but the local vets will know of them. These charities can often provide short and long-term foster homes, especially in an emergency. Phone around and explain your problem. The whole topic of dealing with the deceased's pet is discussed in Chapter 23.

If you are absolutely desperate, one unconventional solution might be to approach the local minister of religion. He may be able to recommend a trusted parishioner who will come in to feed and clean the animal, possibly a pensioner who would welcome the task. In this way, although you are allowing a stranger access to the premises – something normally not to be recommended – at least this person is a known quantity. It is not an ideal solution but it is worth thinking about.

## Religion

Unless the deceased had an antipathy to organized religion and specified a non-religious funeral, it is likely that you have already contacted the appropriate minister. Don't forget that if the deceased had an involvement with a church, synagogue or mosque, he might also have belonged to specific religious groups. The minister of religion will know this, but it may not occur to him that you don't have this information unless you specifically mention it.

## State

Official documents are evidence of the deceased's life and legal status and it is absolutely crucial that you don't part with these. The one exception is the passport. This must be returned – recorded delivery – to the Passport Office, Clive House, Petty France, London SW1H 9HD. Put the other documents somewhere safe where they cannot be lost, stolen or have coffee spilt on them.

## Transport

Make sure that any transport owned by the deceased which is not in a garage is legal – a car without tax, MOT and insurance cannot, for example, be parked on a public road.

## Travel

Don't forget to return any season tickets and obtain a refund. If the deceased had an unused airline ticket, see if you can find out which travel agent issued it, or phone the airline's desk at the airport: you might be able to get a refund in some circumstances.

## Utilities

In addition to arranging for bills to be paid don't forget that there must be a final reading if you need to vacate the premises, and in these circumstances certain utilities such as gas, electricity and telephone need to be disconnected.

When you have been through all the papers, assigned them to their proper files and made short notes of the action you need to take in each case, you are ready to start writing letters. (Sample letters which cover most situations are given in Appendix 4.)

# 11

# Turning Detective

Unless the deceased was exceptionally tidy and organized, you may find there are certain documents you cannot discover among his personal effects. No doubt the deceased knew exactly where to put his hands on them, but you are mystified. What do you do? It is also unfortunately quite common for the deceased's family and friends to realize that there are relatives who need to be contacted, but for whom you have no current address. This may be because they are named in the will as beneficiaries, or simply because they have a moral right to know that a death has taken place. Typically, this is where the deceased had children who have moved away and drifted out of contact or where a family has been scattered because of emigration or a domestic feud. In some cases you might have a legal obligation to try to find these people. In other cases you might feel morally obliged at least to make the attempt. Where do you start?

The infuriating thing is that someone, somewhere will have the information you want: just think of the information held on computer because everyone has a medical card or a National Insurance number. The trouble is, this information is inaccessible to the man in the street. You need to tackle some of these problems from another angle.

## ❶ Find Out Exactly What Documents Are Missing

Chapter 10 explains how you can reduce the papers left by the deceased to a coherent form. You may well find when you have done this that the missing document turns up, probably in an unlikely place. How often do you put something down in the kitchen or in the bedroom simply because that was where you were when you last looked at it? Of course, you were intending to file it away, but somehow it never got done. If death intervenes, it never will get filed away and this can present a problem for the people left behind. So don't assume that because something is not in its logical place that it is missing. Wait until you have allocated each document you can lay your hands on to its proper file, otherwise you will waste time and energy searching for something that may well turn up. If, after this, a document is still missing, you can then think about taking other steps to find it.

## ⓣ Go Back to Source

The trick to finding missing documents is to remember that somewhere there will be a record or a copy of that document. All you need do is work out where the parent record is held. Sometimes, just contacting the organization holding the parent record and sending a copy of the death certificate is enough. It is impossible in a book of this size to go through every individual possibility, but some examples will give you the general idea.

### Driving licence

Write to the DVLC in Swansea (address in Appendix 5), who retain details of all current driving licences on computer. You will need to do this anyway to inform them of the deceased's death, but in your letter explain that you cannot find the original, and give all the details you can, including date and place of birth and the car registration number if you have it. Include a copy of the death certificate. Take a photocopy of this letter.

### Building society book

If you have reason to believe the deceased kept an account at a building society, write to them or visit them in person. You will need the personal details of the deceased, a copy of the death certificate and of the will (or grant of probate). You do not need to go into tremendous detail as to why you think the deceased had an account there: the fact that you have legal status to ask these questions is enough. They will check their computerized records to tell you whether there is an account and how much is in it.

### Title deeds to the house

First of all, try the deceased's bank or solicitor. If this fails, contact the local building societies. This is where you have to use a little cunning. In most cases it is reasonable to assume that the deceased will have used a building society with a branch near to where he lived, so go through the local Yellow Pages. However, there may be circumstances where this does not apply. The deceased may have used a broker and the mortgage might be held by an organization miles away. Work though all the local brokers in Yellow Pages and look among his effects for letters or an address.

## Miscellaneous contacts

This is where you find out that most detective work is tedious. If you think, for example, that the deceased might have used a local aromatherapist and you can find no record of this, the only thing you can do is to go through the telephone directory entry by entry asking whether they had a patient by that name.

## ⓣ Find Missing Persons

This is surprisingly difficult. It is extremely hard for people actually to disappear without trace as they will leave a trail of computer records, but most of these will be closed to you. You have to approach the problem through the back door. There are several possibilities.

ⓗ   Write down absolutely everything you know about the missing person on a piece of paper. Phone or write to anyone who knew him and ask them to do the same thing. Reduce all this information to a series of facts and possible leads.

### Salvation Army

This organization runs a low-cost operation to find missing people and has an extraordinarily high success rate of about seventy-five per cent. The fact that the person you are seeking may have been out of contact for some time is irrelevant – their typical request is to search for someone who has been out of contact for seventeen years.

To use the service you will need to fill in a fairly detailed form and have a personal interview. The way their Family Tracing Service works is that when they locate the person, they will approach him and ask whether he is willing to be put back in contact. The address of that person will never be given out unless he agrees. If the person is interested but cautious, for whatever reason, the Family Tracing Service runs a 'mail box' which allows the relatives to exchange letters to see if both want the initial contact to turn into something more personal. They are also quite happy to handle enquiries if you believe the person has moved abroad.

There is, however, a snag. The service is only for the purpose of reuniting families for emotional reasons, to encourage reconciliation between families, and there are certain categories of enquiries they will not touch, and these are:

- Friends. A legal relationship must exist before the Tracing

Service will handle the case. You may want to contact the deceased's army buddies but you will have to find another way to do this.

- People under the age of seventeen. This is simply because the search methods the Tracing Services uses are not effective in these cases.

- The natural parent of an adopted or illegitimate child.

- A husband or wife being sought for divorce proceedings.

- Any relative if the reason for the search is for estate, legal or business purposes.

- Common-law partners, co-habitees or fiancés.

At first sight this list would seem to rule out any chance of the Tracing Service taking your case. However, speak to them about it. If you only want to find someone because they are named in the will and you have no personal interest in them the Service will not act. However, the death might have made you aware that you, or the missing person, could also die before any reconciliation takes place. If you can convince the Tracing Service that this is your reason, they may be prepared to act.

## The Public Record Office

The good news is that all public records have to be lodged there. The bad news is that there are extremely restrictive rules about what you can see. But why should these records be of any use when you are tracing someone? It all goes back to sleuthing.

You may not have heard from someone for a number of years, but there are certain events that happen to most people during that time. They might get married, divorced, have a child, change their name, or even die. All this information is recorded by the state. The trouble is, you cannot get at the most recent records: most are held back from the general public until a certain number of years have passed. This period differs in each case but in general it is over thirty years. (The address of the Public Record Office is given in Appendix 5.)

This doesn't make it a waste of time to look through these records. First, if the person has indeed been missing a long time you might find a new starting point for your search – if a birth is registered to him, you will know when it took place and where, and the mother's name. This means you can focus your search on that geographical area, perhaps by working out how old the child is, and contacting schools, or speaking to local ministers of religion. Second, by going back to some of the earlier information, you might find facts you did not otherwise know.

## Shipping records

If you believe that the person emigrated, there is a reasonable chance that you can find him by browsing through the records of the different shipping lines. There will be a passenger list for each ship which left a UK port and provided the missing person sailed under his own name, you may be able to track him down at least to a particular country.

## Private detectives

Your best bet, even if it is the most expensive, is to hire a private detective. As already explained, there is a massive amount of information on each of us somewhere on file which is not accessible to the general public. Many private detectives, though, are ex-policemen and they may well have personal contacts which enable them to tap into the system. There has been much written in the press recently about the ease with which some of these detectives can obtain information and provided you can give them a starting point, you have a reasonable chance of success.

There are also specialist agencies which deal with enquiries related to wills. These sometimes base their fees on a proportion of the amount to be inherited, or otherwise quote a fee per hour plus expenses, depending on the situation.

## Advertising in the press

If you need to find someone because he has inherited money but the sum is not sufficient to make it worth hiring a private detective, you must make an effort to find him and the best way is to advertise in the press. Put an ad in the paper of the district in which he last lived – he may no longer be there but someone might remember him. It is also wise, if only to cover your own back, to place an advertisement in a national paper. Don't go into long explanations as to why you want to find him. It might be an idea to use a solicitor as an intermediary, so that the missing person can contact him first and find out why he is being sought. Also, check out any replies carefully. Missing people are often sought because of provisions in wills, and if you respond too freely with your name and address, you might find you attract too much attention from someone rather unsavoury.

The basic message is that most missing people can be found. It all depends how much you are willing to spend to make this happen.

# 12

# Disposing of Personal Effects

You may be left with some or all of the deceased's possessions which you need to dispose of. These can range from the suit he has had hanging in the wardrobe for the last twenty years to his collection of unpublished short stories, or a brand new microwave. What do you do with them? Someone, somewhere will want them, but how do you proceed? Most interesting of all, what are these things worth?

## ❶ Check Your Legal Situation

As explained in more detail in Chapters 13 to 16, you cannot, in many cases, blithely start throwing things out, selling them or giving them away as soon as the death has taken place.

## ❶ Decide What You Want to Dispose Of

You have to be realistic about this. The deceased may have had very different interests and tastes to yours. Just because something belonged to him doesn't mean you are going to use that item again, and unless it has special sentimental value, all it is going to do is to take up space in your own home. The temptation is to hang on to everything: disposing of the deceased's possessions is like losing him all over again. You simply cannot do this unless you live in a mansion. Moreover, there are other factors to think about. Unused clothes, for example, can attract moths, and moths are not discriminating: once they have worked their way through the deceased's possessions packed away at the top of the wardrobe they will start on yours.

There are two ways to approach this problem:

- Go through each item and decide whether you want to keep it or not.

- Go through each item assuming you *don't* want to keep it unless there is a very strong reason for doing so.

The second approach will leave you with a far smaller pile to find space for.

**⊕**    Arm yourself with at least a dozen black plastic bin liners. You are certain to need them and it is amazing how quickly they fill up.

## ⊕ Decide What is Likely to Have Real Monetary Value

You need to keep separate these things which you are likely to be able to re-sell for a considerable amount. First, you are going to have to have these properly valued, and second, they will be far easier to dispose of. Items which might go on this pile are antiques (even if you think they are ugly), jewellery, paintings and any kind of collection (old records, etc).

## ⊕ Sell Items of Real Monetary Value For Their Correct Price

The first thing is to get them valued by an expert. If you simply march into the nearest shop with the item under your arm in a paper bag, the chances are the shopkeeper will lick his lips with anticipation at the profit he is about to make. There are innumerable stories in the press about people who sold the dirty old painting in the loft for £10 and then found out (as the person who bought it suspected) that it was worth a fortune. Don't let this happen to you. It is always worth trying to get more than one quote. Compare these before you make any decision.

If the item is insured, check that the insurance policy is still valid: the cover might have ended with the deceased's death. If it is not insured, insure it immediately. You will need to put a value on it for insurance purposes – a guestimate from a local dealer based on a photo or description is better than nothing. Assume the item is valuable and use the highest quote. You may also find that the insurance company will insist on a proper valuation before they will offer cover; in this case, ask them who they recommend. This might solve a lot of your problems.

### Antiques

Anything which is over about fifty years old is likely to have some kind of value, as long as it is in good condition. What is good condition? It depends on the item and its age. If it is a 200-year-old silver teapot, the odd scratch will reduce its value but it will still be worth quite a lot. The hall table inherited by the deceased from Aunty Maud, which was made in 1930 and now has woodworm, on the other hand, might only be fit for firewood.

Go to a reputable antique dealer or, better still, more than one, and have the item valued. If you think it has great value, contact Christie's or Sotheby's auction rooms in London (addresses in Appendix 5) or another more local auction house. They will need to see the item – photos are no good – so this might mean a journey for you, but if the item has value its sale will more than cover the cost and it will be an interesting day out for you at a time when pleasure is in short supply. Don't think auctioneers always deal in items worth a fortune – they have been known to hold sales of, for example, old comics.

Wherever you go, try not to part with the item. If the antiques dealer says he needs to speak to his expert who is not there at the moment, or will look at it later, offer to come back. If you do decide to part with it, which is not advised, make absolutely sure you have a photo of it and a signed receipt from the dealer.

## Jewellery

The same comments apply. Go to a reputable jeweller dealing in expensive items, not the chain offering low-priced bargains in the High Street. Stand guard over the item. If the dealer should be unscrupulous you might hand over something worth a fortune and get back a cheap imitation. How can you then prove that this is not what you handed in?

## Furniture

Don't try to get potentially valuable furniture assessed by the local house clearance company – they will have no idea of its real value, and if they do you might well not hear the truth. Instead, they might offer to take the item off your hands for a tenner. Go to a dealer. If you can't find one locally, phone one of the big auction houses in London and ask if they can recommend someone.

## Rare items

If the deceased has left something unusual, for example, a Chinese vase he picked up in the Far East when he was a young lad in the army, you would be well advised to go to one of the auction houses in London. A local antiques dealer, if you are lucky enough to find one who can offer an opinion on it, might not appreciate the price it could fetch in an auction open to people throughout the world, although he might be a good starting point to establish that it is, indeed, valuable.

**Ⓗ**   If you are feeling generous, why not see if there is a local museum that might appreciate the item?

## Identify any collections

These days, collections of the strangest items have resale value at auction. If the deceased was a collector, this may be obvious – he might have catalogued things or have them in glass cases or cardboard boxes. However, keep an eye out for several items of the same kind which are scattered around the house. The deceased may not have set out to start a collection but might have accumulated enough over the years for you to put them together and sell them as one.

To see if these items have value, look for specialist shops or societies. Magazines are a good source of information for these: most hobbies support one or more magazines and enthusiasts will often advertise in them. Alternatively, approach one of the London auction houses.

**Ⓗ**   The reference section of your local library will have a book which contains a list of all the magazines on the market. Alternatively, approach the magazine section of a chain of newsagents and ask them what they know of in that subject area.

Don't reject the idea that items may have value because they look like trash, or because they were common in your day. You may remember the time when Dinky Toys could be bought for sixpence: a collection of them might well be worth quite a lot nowadays. Equally, early editions of comics can each have a surprising value to comics collectors: that first edition of the *Beano* you found under the wardrobe may be worth more than you could imagine.

## The car

This is by far the easiest task to undertake. A reputable garage – not the two lads operating from a shed down the local alley – will give you a quote based on its book value (a list of what each car is worth based on the date it was manufactured). This may vary, according to the condition of the car.

**Ⓗ**   Buy a copy of a magazine such as *Exchange and Mart*, or *Used Car Buyer* to get a feel for prices in case someone tries to take advantage of your ignorance.

Don't forget that the car may have originally been purchased under an easy terms agreement or with a bank loan. Liaise with these people about what you intend to do.

### ● Call in a House Clearance Firm, But Carefully!

You may decide, after you have weeded out the items of obvious value, that you really cannot be bothered with selling each item separately. One solution is to phone a local auction house: the other is to call in a house clearance firm. There will certainly be one near to you and you will also find them advertising in the local paper.

You should know three things:

- You will not be offered much. They need to make a profit on the sale of second-hand items so the amount they offer you might seem derisory. Consider, though, that they will collect and this does at least save you a great deal of physical effort.

- Some of these firms are surprisingly fussy, especially if you live in an area where there are wealthy families living locally. Why should they bother trying to sell that old wardrobe the deceased bought from a chain store when the house down the road has offered them top of the range furniture? If they are interested in some of the deceased's items but not others, make it a condition of sale that to get the items they want, they have to take the lot.

- Many of these house clearance firms are reputable and honest. Some are not. These firms will have no scruples about offering you pence for something which is quite valuable. You should also beware of people advertising house clearance as a cover for burglary. They ask people to phone them so they can give a quote for the job, get the name of the deceased's house then call round that night with an empty lorry. You may have solved your house clearance problem, but you will have received no money and you will have to spend time with the police giving details of the burglary. Make sure the firm has some kind of shop at least, so you know where it can be found. Also, ask locally if it is reputable.

**H** One useful way of finding a good firm is to ask a bank manager or solicitor: they may well have had feedback on which firms to use and which to avoid.

## ❶ Decide What is Junk

This is where you might have a rude awakening if you try to dispose of items individually. Unless something is collectable (antiques, etc), it will probably be worth next to nothing. This category covers the deceased's furniture, clothes, books and electrical goods. So what do you do? You can:

- Give it away.
- Sell it (see above).
- Throw it away.

Each presents problems.

### Giving Things Away

It is astonishing but true that when there are so many families in desperate need in this country it is hard to find someone to accept second-hand items.

### Charity shops

The obvious thing to do is to go to your local charity shop. You can head straight for Oxfam, or you can check to see whether your favourite charity also has a shop in the area – many people forget about this possibility when under stress. The Red Cross, various cancer and animal charities and the YMCA have shops nationwide, to mention just a few. Check in your local phone directory or take a walk around town one afternoon.

Remember, though, that these shops are there to make money for the charity. They will not take anything unsaleable or in poor condition. You may think they would be glad of that blanket with a stain on it but you might be surprised. Someone, somewhere will want it, for a certainty, but you have to find another way of reaching them.

Many of these charity shops will collect, provided you give them time to make arrangements.

### Charitable organizations

There are many charitable organizations dealing directly with deprived families who will be only too glad to take the deceased's possessions. Organizations you might want to think about are refuges for battered women, drug abuse centres, refugee centres and those run by religious associations. There are a number of these but the Society of St Vincent de Paul will have branches in most towns and cities and will take anything they can possibly use, and send the deceased's possessions directly to people in need. You will find the address of your nearest branch in the telephone directory.

## The church

Many churches will know of families in need or, if they have the space, will store items for when they are approached by someone who is in financial straits. If they do not, they will know of the organizations associated with that church who will be glad to hear from you.

## Jumble sales

Many local charities and fund-raising groups will run jumble sales and will advertise these in the paper. Go around some of these and speak to the organizers, asking if they are interested in some of the deceased's possessions and the kind of things they can sell.

### Things That Are Hard To Give Away

You will find it difficult to give away electrical goods of any kind, especially to a charity shop. This is for two reasons:

- The organization taking the item cannot know beyond all doubt that it is safe, and therefore cannot accept the liability of reselling it.

- EC Regulations mean that much electrical equipment now fails to meet certain European standards and thus cannot legally be put on sale.

As always, however, someone, somewhere will want them. You may well find a house clearance company which will take them, although you will almost certainly not be happy about what you will be offered.

The alternative is to approach a charitable organization, like the St Vincent de Paul Society. They may well know of a family to whom a washing machine would be a gift beyond price.

Be charitable yourself. Pay to have the item checked over unless it is relatively new and you know it is in good condition: you would not want to be responsible for a fire caused by an electrical fault in something you gave away. Think of the cost of this as an extra gift from the deceased to someone in need. If you really can't afford to do this or don't have the time – perhaps you live in another part of the country – explain the situation to the organization and let them decide whether they want to take the item or not.

## Computers

Surprisingly, certain computers are just as hard to dispose of as electrical items. This is, of course, because technology has progressed so much and old computers are valueless. Try advertising in your local newspaper. You may, however, have to accept that you have yet another item for the refuse tip.

## Throwing Things Away

Don't forget that you cannot just stack a ten foot high pile of junk next to the dustbin and expect the refuse collectors to take it. At the very least you will have to put things in black plastic sacks.

You may find the refuse collectors will refuse to take these sacks if there are too many of them at any one time. The answer is either to phone the Refuse Collection Department of the Local Authority and make a special arrangement, or take them to the council tip.

If you want to throw out furniture or large items, it is essential to check the situation: some councils will send a lorry to collect these but others prohibit items like these being left on the streets.

### ❶ Hold a Garage Sale/Car Boot Sale

Both are excellent ways of disposing of miscellaneous items you don't want. Garage sales have the advantage of enabling you to move the possessions out of the house to give yourself some space. Car boot sales are held almost every weekend. You need to pay a minimal amount – often under £10 – to buy yourself a pitch, but you can clear a considerable number of items in this way. You will find them advertised in the local paper.

**❶** Take something with which to make a table on which to display the goods, or a rug to lay on the ground. Buy a large sheet of transparent plastic to throw over these in case it rains to save you putting them back into the car while a short shower passes over.

Never think of holding an auction actually inside the house. This is an invitation to burglars and people with light fingers.

### ❶ Keep Souvenirs and Mementoes Safe

If you decide to keep all the deceased's items which have sentimental value, such as his collection of photos, make sure they are put in a safe place. You are unlikely to look at them or use them on a regular basis and their condition can deteriorate over time, in which case there was little point in keeping them in the first place.

### ❶ Find a Home For the Deceased's Religious Items

Many people will keep some item related to their religion in their home, perhaps a crucifix or a prayer book. Even if you are not religious it might well seem wrong simply to toss these in the dustbin.

They will almost certainly have no resale value even if you can find an outlet. However, your local minister of religion may be willing to take them for a fund-raising event, or know of a pensioner who would be glad to possess such an item but cannot afford it.

If you are determined, you should be able to find a home for any of the deceased's items you don't want to keep. It is well worth thinking about giving them to charity as the money you are likely to receive is going to be low, but if that money is going to be important to you, ask around and see what you are offered before making any decisions.

# Part III

# *Money*

## Introduction and Warning

This section deals with wills and the administration of an estate.

In the majority of instances there will be absolutely no problem with this, especially where there is a surviving spouse or the estate is uncomplicated. However, you always need to be careful when dealing with money or property, and especially when this involves the law.

Most people should find administration of an estate a relatively easy, if time-consuming task. Common-sense will tell you, however, that no book sold to the general public can contain an explanation of all the legal problems that can crop up in any imaginable situation. You will only find this information in legal textbooks, which are expensive and probably totally incomprehensible to the average person.

The best practical advice is to consult a solicitor if you have the slightest doubt about what you are doing, and in certain circumstances which will be explained in the chapters that follow.

Don't forget that you can still handle many matters yourself. You do not have to pay a solicitor to do everything. It is perfectly acceptable to go to a solicitor to get advice on one or two points, and to deal with other matters without his aid.

By doing this, and for only a relatively small sum of money, you may avoid doing something which is illegal or which will get you into a mess with the Inland Revenue.

You might find it helpful to know that solicitors' fees vary greatly. If you need to seek advice, phone up, explain what you want and ask how much he will charge. If he is not prepared to give you at least some idea, phone another solicitor.

Don't forget, also, that you can obtain advice from a Citizen's Advice Bureau or a Law Centre, and that will cost you nothing at all.

The rule to remember is – when in doubt, seek advice!

# 13

# The Will

Many people feel that it is a sign of disrespect to start thinking about the will immediately after a death. After all, shouldn't money should be the last thing on your mind at the moment? You're not some kind of vulture, picking over the leavings at the earliest opportunity. No, putting off the search for the will shows you are grieving, or at the very least is a sign of respect for the deceased. Even when you finally mention the 'W' word there is a faint sense of unease. Are you appearing too keen to find out more about its contents? Are you showing an unseemly interest in who is to receive the deceased's money and possessions?

This attitude is deeply ingrained in most of us and is wholly understandable. For one thing, reading the will reinforces the fact that the deceased is actually dead: you would never be allowed such intimate access to his financial affairs during his life. There is also the pressure to 'do the right thing'. Even if you were not close to the deceased (perhaps he was an uncle you hardly knew), you must demonstrate to everyone involved that he matters more than his possessions. You do this by allowing a few days to elapse before you start on mundane tasks. It is a sign that you are too grief-stricken to think about anything but the deceased. You might, indeed, be genuinely too grief-stricken to cope.

Another reason to put off thinking about the will is that you are stepping into an area involving the law and legal terminology, which can make the whole business seem a bit daunting. After all, what exactly is an executor or an administrator, and what is the difference? What is a grant of probate and how on earth do you go about getting one?

Whatever the reason, it is the wrong way to react. If you feel other friends and relations might comment adversely on your mercenary approach, ignore them. You might be the one named in the will to sort out the deceased's estate. If something goes wrong because of your delay, you, not they, would have to bear the consequences. And if you are too grief-stricken to care about such things at the moment, remember that the will might contain instructions from the deceased about his funeral. You need to know this as soon as possible in order to make the necessary arrangements. The tradition advocated on television and in crime novels of reading the will after the funeral is a recipe for disaster.

You certainly don't have to worry about not understanding legal words and phrases. All those you are likely to come across are explained in this chapter. There is also information on how to check that the will is valid, and any likely problems in its content.

## Some Terms You Will Find Helpful

Unfamiliar words and phrases can be off-putting and make it difficult for you to understand what you are reading. The following are terms that are going to crop up repeatedly and unavoidably in the next few chapters, and they are explained in a way which, hopefully, takes away the mystique.

| | |
|---|---|
| Administrator | A person who administers (manages) the deceased's estate. |
| Beneficiary | A person who is left something in a will. |
| Bequest | The gift a beneficiary receives. |
| Codicil | A legal addition to a will. |
| Co-habitee | A non-married partner. |
| Estate | The money, property and possessions the deceased leaves behind. |
| Executor/ Executrix | A person named in the deceased's will who is tasked with managing the deceased's estate in accordance with his stated wishes. |
| Intestate | Where there is no will, or no valid will. |
| Legacy | A gift of money or particular items. |
| Probate | A court document confirming a will. |
| Trust | A fund set apart in the deceased's estate to be used for a particular purpose |
| Trustee | A person who manages a trust. |
| Residue | The balance of somebody's estate after paying debts, giving away legacies etc. |

## ❶ Find the Will

If you are absolutely sure there is no will, turn to page 153: there is a special set of rules governing this situation, and you should know about them.

If you believe there is, or might be, a will in existence you must do your best to find it, and be seen to do your best. There are certain places where you should search and certain people you should ask to see if it can be located.

- See if the deceased has made a record of where it is kept – this information might be in a diary or on a computer. If the person is elderly he might have used one of the excellent forms produced by Age Concern, on which he can record useful information, such as the whereabouts of the will.

- Look among his personal papers: people often keep their important documents in one place, so if you know where, for example, the deeds to the house are kept, this would be a likely place to look.

- Check with his solicitor. You should be able to find his details from the deceased's address book. Alternatively, look among his papers for letters from his solicitor, the heading of which will give you the information you need.

- Ask the deceased's bank(s) if it is lodged there, or if they have knowledge of it.

- The deceased may have approached someone and asked him to act as executor. See if you can discover who this might be – try family members and close friends – and ask if they have any information as to whether a will was ever drawn up and where it might be kept.

If this fails to produce results, you must start to look further afield.

- Check with other solicitors in the area. The deceased might have used more than one firm – he might, for example, have needed specialist advice his normal solicitor couldn't supply – or he might have changed his solicitor without updating his address book.

- Check with Somerset House (address in Appendix 5). Wills can be lodged there for a small fee and the deceased may have felt this was the safe and (to him) obvious thing to do.

- Advertise in the local paper, asking for information. It is also an extremely good idea to place an advert in one of the magazines aimed specifically at lawyers, like the *Law Society Gazette* (address in Appendix 5). Hopefully you will gain useful information, but you are also covering yourself against the possible charge that you did not hunt as hard as you might have done for the will.

If you still haven't found the will you need to see a solicitor, as it may be that the deceased will be deemed to have died intestate (without making a will), even if you are sure one exists.

## ⊤ Decide If the Will is Valid

Let us assume you have now found the will. Your first task is to decide whether or not it is valid.

If it was drawn up by the deceased's solicitor, it should be in order. The solicitor will have ensured that it was prepared in the proper way, is correctly signed and witnessed and that it contains nothing which is going to invalidate it.

There is, however, no law that says that a solicitor has to be involved in the drawing up of a will. It might be that the deceased drew it up himself at home using one of the 'will packs' that are on the market. He might have asked his solicitor to cast an eye over it to check that everything was correct, but it is perfectly possible that it has never been seen by anyone but himself.

If you see it is a home-made will, don't immediately panic and assume you have trouble on your hands. Many of the home will kits are very well laid out with clear instructions as to what to do and what not to do. Provided the deceased followed these instructions properly, it should be a perfectly valid will which is not going to cause any difficulties for you or for anyone else. However, it is a good idea to have it double-checked by a solicitor, especially if the will is complex or unclear, or large amounts of money or property are involved.

If you feel this is an extra task you could well do without, and perhaps to your horror feel slightly exasperated with the deceased for not having used a solicitor in the first place, remember that he was obviously trying to do the right thing. He had good intentions in that he took the trouble to draw up the will at all. Many, many people don't bother to do so, and this can cause enormous distress to those left behind.

### What is a Will?

A will is a document in which the deceased states what he wants done with his money, property and possessions after his death, and which, in order to be valid, is drawn up in accordance with certain legal requirements. In the overwhelming majority of cases, once you know what to look for it will be immediately obvious whether or not these requirements are met. The things to check are:

- That the deceased was over eighteen when he made the will. The will should be dated in either the opening lines or at the bottom, so you can work this out quickly and easily:

- That the deceased was of sound mind when he made the will. That doesn't automatically mean that if he was on anti-depressants, or was in a mental home, you are going to have problems. As long as medical opinion can show that the deceased understood what he was doing, the will should stand.

- That the deceased hadn't remarried since he made the will. It might sound incredible but remarriage automatically invalidates an existing will unless the will specifically states that it is made in contemplation of a particular forthcoming marriage and that it will not be revoked by that marriage. The reason, when you think about it, is quite sound – a new marriage means new commitments and responsibilities, and there is an assumption that the deceased will want to reflect these in his will – therefore, any existing will is invalid.

- That the will must be properly signed and witnessed. The rules are very strict about this, and also about the order in which it was done. The deceased must have arranged for two people to witness the will and he must have signed it (or, if he was unable to sign through some disability, directed someone else to sign for him) in their presence. Then both witnesses must have signed in his presence. It is, of course, going to be immediately obvious if either the deceased or one of the witnesses failed to sign. The will is then obviously invalid, but how do you know if the signing was carried out in the right way? The will itself should tell you. There should be a clause, called an attestation clause, stating exactly how and in what order the signing was carried out. If the attestation clause is not there, don't worry, as this is not going to invalidate the will, but it might cause you problems at a later stage, if you should decide to apply for probate (see page 143). In that case, you will need to get a sworn statement from one of the witnesses showing that the signing procedure was carried out correctly. This is easy enough if the witnesses live in the next street but not so funny if they have both emigrated to Australia without leaving a forwarding address.

**ⓗ** If one or more of the witnesses' signatures is missing, consider whether this might have been intentional rather than an accident. Perhaps the deceased left the formalities uncompleted because he changed his mind about what he had written, made another will at a later date and forgot to destroy this one. In that case, you will have to start hunting for the valid will. You need to rely on your knowledge of the deceased to estimate how likely this is. If he was super-organized, this might be unlikely. Such a person would probably have made sure this draft will was destroyed, but if he was more slapdash in dealing with his affairs, it is a possibility you should consider.

When you have checked that these requirements have been met and that the will is valid, you need to turn your attention to its content.

## ⓣ Read and Understand the Contents of the Will

In theory, a will might contain almost anything but in reality its content is usually limited to the names of executors (people who will manage the deceased's estate after his death), details as to whom he wants to leave his money, property and possessions, and quite often, wishes about his funeral and the disposal of his body. Read the will through. Hopefully, all will be quite clear, but if some of the words and phrases mystify you, turn to page 138 for a lesson on reading and interpreting a will.

### Executors

If the deceased has gone to the trouble of drawing up a will and leaving instructions as to what will happen to his money and property, presumably he will also have thought about who is to administer his estate after his death. In his will he can name someone who is responsible for ensuring that any specific instructions are carried out, and for administering his estate generally. Such a person is called an executor (executrix, if female, though often just the male term is used). It is his duty to make sure that any money owing to the deceased's estate is collected, that all the deceased's debts are paid (and any incurred after his death such as funeral expenses), that all the deceased's affairs are wound up and that all bequests are paid out as he instructed. (The duties of an executor are discussed in greater detail in Chapter 14).

The deceased should have named at least one person: quite often it is two. Naming two is sensible, as being an executor is a time-consuming task which is best shared. The maximum number that can act is four.

Quite often, an executor (or executors) will be family members who have a vested interest in ensuring that things are managed quickly and properly. Typically, this might be the surviving spouse and/or grown-up children, or a brother or sister of the deceased. He may have felt, however, that it would be unfair to place the burden of administering the estate on the shoulders of family members, who would have to cope with their own grief as well as trying to focus on more practical matters. In such circumstances the deceased is likely to have turned to a close friend.

If the deceased has chosen his solicitor to act as executor this should not be seen as a slight on his family and friends, rather as an act of kindness in wishing to take the burden off their shoulders.

It is important to find out who the executor is (or are) as soon as possible as someone has to make sure enough money is available to pay for the funeral, and there may be other urgent tasks that need to be carried out. If it is you who have been named as executor, read pages 143 to 144 to find out exactly what your duties are. If it is not you, be sure not to do anything without the approval of the executor, especially if it involves money or property, or you might find yourself personally liable for the consequences.

## Bequests

These are gifts from the deceased of money, property or personal possessions to people of his choice. They can be of little monetary value or they can be worth a great deal. Hopefully, the recipients of the bequests will attach more importance to their sentimental value and the fact that the deceased cared enough to remember them, than to their market value.

Human nature being what it is, things may not work out this way. All too often, the friends and relatives of someone who has died react strongly when they find out they have been left less than anticipated, or nothing at all. As you read through the will, keep an eye out for any bequests which might cause problems. You should be aware that in some circumstances it is possible to challenge a will on the grounds that someone has received an insufficient share of the deceased's estate. However, these circumstances are quite specific (see page 136) and in most cases all that will happen is a certain amount of grumbling and discontent. If you know the person causing trouble has no grounds on which to claim, you can ignore him.

Even if the will is clear and valid, none of the bequests should be paid out immediately, as the estate has to be valued and the deceased's debts paid. It is also likely that probate will have to be applied for in order for the estate to be administered at all. If these points seem a little unclear at this stage, don't worry – they will be explained in greater detail in the following chapters. The important thing to remember if you have just read the deceased's will is not to give things away or sell them at this stage.

## Interests for life or a specified period

There is one point that might need explanation. It is possible – and legal – for the deceased to give someone the use of something during his lifetime or for a specified period. This doesn't mean he owns it in the sense of being able to sell it or dump it on the Council refuse tip. One example of this might be where Great Aunt Annie has had the use of the deceased's grand piano for some time because she can't afford to buy one of her own. In his will the deceased might, as an act of kindness, instruct that she can have the use of this grand piano for the rest of her life.

When Great Aunt Annie dies, however, the grand piano will not form part of her estate because she does not own it: all she has had is a kind of extended loan of the piano. That means she cannot decide in her will to whom it should go next. That decision will already have been made by the deceased in his will. Having given the use of it to Great Aunt Annie for the duration of her life, he will have stated that on her death ownership of the piano should pass to a person he names. So Great Aunt Annie has no say in the ultimate fate of the piano. Note, however, that the value of the piano is included in any inheritance tax calculations on the deceased's estate, even though Great Aunt Annie has possession and use of it for her lifetime.

## Gifts to charity

It is quite common for someone to leave a sum of money to a named charity in his will. If the deceased has done this you may find his choice of charity helpful should you decide you want donations rather than flowers at his funeral. He might also have instructed that if some or all of the people to whom he has left a bequest die before him, their share of the estate should go to this charity. If it seems that the part of the deceased's estate which he wanted to go to charity is going to be sizeable, it might be a good idea to contact the charity or charities concerned so that if it or they would like to take some of the deceased's assets rather than the proceeds of selling them, this may be possible.

### Where a beneficiary dies before the deceased

Hopefully, the deceased should have considered a worst-case scenario, in which one or all of the beneficiaries dies before him. There will often be a chain of instructions, stating who a beneficiary is, then saying that if the latter should predecease him, that particular gift will then go to a specified person or organization.

### Funeral Instructions

The deceased might have left instructions in his will as to how, where and when he wants the funeral to take place, and whether he wants to be buried or cremated. He might have expressed a general wish, perhaps a preference for burial, or his instructions might be much more detailed, down to the route the funeral cortège should take and the minister who is to conduct the service. Clearly, you will want to do your best to carry these out. How to do this is explained in Chapter 7.

### Medical instructions

It is also possible that the deceased will have requested his body be used for research, or parts of it be used for transplants. If the deceased leaves a spouse or partner it is likely that this is something they would have discussed. However, it may be that this comes as a surprise to the surviving partner, who reacts with revulsion. You must handle this situation with extreme care, balancing the wishes of the deceased against those of the partner.

As far as transplants are concerned, if you are reading the will it is almost certainly too late for donation to be possible: organs for donation need to be removed from the body almost immediately after death. Unfortunately, many people with good intentions do not understand this, and so their organs, which they would very much like to have donated to help keep another person alive and in good health, cannot be used. See Chapter 22 for more information on this subject.

If you feel you are honour bound to do something to carry out the spirit of the deceased's wishes, you might want to consider a personal donation to one of the medical research charities instead. You can get the names of these charities from the reference section of your local library.

### Trusts

You might see from the wording of the will that money or property is to be held in trust for someone. This means that the deceased wants to give that person a gift, but not directly. Typically, this might be where the deceased wants to give a reasonably large sum of money to a child who is too young to look after his own affairs. (The deceased might also have sensibly decided that access to large sums of money at too young an age is usually a recipe for disaster.)

What the deceased might have done in this situation is to place the money into the hands of a trustee, who will be specifically named in the will. That trustee will look after this gift for the child until, for example, he reaches his eighteenth (or other specified) birthday. Until that time the trustee must usually do all in his power to prevent the value of the gift from decreasing or disappearing, and should try to increase its total worth. (There are lots of rules about how a trustee goes about this, but that is a specialized area of law.) During the period in which he holds the gift in trust the trustee might, typically, pay a small sum to the child at regular intervals or be able to purchase essential items such as a computer, if he feels this is important and useful. The child, on his eighteenth (or other specified) birthday, will inherit the full sum and the trust will be ended.

Exactly what the trustees' instructions are will be detailed in the will, and these will vary from case to case. One thing is certain: the trustees themselves cannot make a profit out of the money or property. However, where a professional such as a solicitor, accountant or bank is appointed to act as a trustee they may, if the will so provides, be able to cover their normal professional charges.

You might well ask why the deceased did not, in the example given above, just give the money to the parents and let them hand it over to the child on his eighteenth birthday. Surely creating a trust is somewhat insulting? Far from it. The deceased has done them a favour. It is easy to imagine circumstances in which the parents decide to use some of the money in an emergency – perhaps the father has been thrown out of work and they are in arrears with the mortgage. There might be a genuine intention to pay the money back as soon as possible, but what if this can't be done? What the deceased has prevented by setting up the trust is a conflict of interest. The parents don't have access to the money and therefore cannot spend it, and this saves them from possible recriminations later.

Trusts come in all shapes and sizes, and do not have to involve children. Remember, if you find you have been named as a trustee, it shows the deceased had great faith in your honesty.

If you have just read a will, seen a trust has been set up and thrown up your hands in horror at the trustee named, you should know that in some circumstances it is possible to dismiss a trustee, but you do need to consult a solicitor for this.

## ❶ Scan the Will Specifically For Any Problems it May Contain

The next section is not intended to frighten you, but you do need to know the kind of things that can be wrong with the wording of a will. Most wills drawn up by solicitors or with their input should be problem-free, as are many wills drawn up at home. However, it would be misleading to pretend that problems can't occur. If they do, the consequences can be serious. For one thing, an executor who misinterprets a will or ignores something that is wrong with it will have to face the consequences of his actions. It is absolutely essential to ensure that nothing is wrong with the will which can cause problems at a later stage.

If you were to go to your local library, take out a book on wills and look at all the different cases in which something has gone wrong, you would be horrified: it might seem as if it is almost impossible to draw up a trouble-free will, especially without a solicitor. However, it is rather like looking at a medical textbook and becoming convinced that you must have the symptoms for at least one of the diseases described there. The cases described in the lawbook are the interesting cases, the ones that define what should and should not be done. A solicitor knows about these, as do the people who have drawn up the instructions for the home will kit, basing their instructions on this knowledge. Anyone who follows these instructions and is disposing of the kind of estate an average person might own should have made a valid, uncomplicated will.

If you have a will which hasn't been seen by a solicitor, you might find this list helpful in deciding whether or not to bring one in. The list has been divided into two categories – things which should send you straight to a solicitor, and things which should cause you to question.

Things which should send you straight to a solicitor

- If the will isn't dated. The date on which the will was signed should be there somewhere, usually in the opening lines or at the end. If it isn't, it doesn't invalidate the will but you will have some difficulties if you need to apply for probate.

- Complex bequests. If the deceased has drawn up the will himself, warning bells should sound if there are complex bequests, particularly those involving large amounts of money or property. It is all too easy for a non-lawyer to use the wrong words.

- Ambiguous wording. The same applies if you read through the will and it isn't clear what the deceased is saying, or if any part of it is capable of more than one meaning;

- Things can become very complicated where there is a foreign element, for example, property owned abroad, or where the deceased was resident abroad. At first sight you might think this would apply only to the super-rich, but this country contains a considerable number of people who are immigrants or the offspring of immigrants. A good example of how this might affect an ordinary family is where an Irish or perhaps Bangladeshi immigrant, resident in England, has bought a small piece of land 'back home'. Another is where the deceased had some stocks and shares and some of them can only be sold on a foreign exchange.

- When there is any mention of a property other than a straight bequest of the family home to the spouse. That is not to say you will automatically have problems if property is involved but there are potential pitfalls here.

- When there are complicated family relationships. Bequests to divorced or separated spouses, or attempts to exclude them from inheriting, need to be worded carefully. Again, this is not necessarily going to cause you a problem but, especially if the deceased drew up the will himself, check it out.

- When there are any alterations to the text of the will. Unless the alteration has also been clearly signed by the deceased and the two witnesses (even their initials will do), alterations made after signing don't count.

- When there are assets of more than £200,000. The reason for this is that estates worth more than this attract Inheritance Tax. This is something that definitely needs the attention of a lawyer even if you feel competent to work out how much tax is due, as there are legal ways in some circumstances to ease the tax burden.

- When there is a likelihood that the estate is insolvent.

- When there is any mention of a trust.

## Things which should cause you to question

- If the will is witnessed by someone also named as executor, or someone named as a beneficiary. When this happens, the problem is theirs rather than yours. The will is still valid but the person will not be able to claim any money from the estate. (In the case of an executor he will not even be able to claim expenses incurred in managing the estate.) The same applies if one of the witnesses is the spouse of a beneficiary. If the deceased hasn't realized there is a problem here, you might want to ask yourself what else he has missed.

- Legal terminology. Watch out for this if the deceased drew up the will without a solicitor. Legal words and phrases, like fireworks, are fine if used in the right place at the right time: use them wrongly and you may well have trouble. The deceased may have used legal terminology on the assumption that it somehow made the will more 'official'. This is a mistaken belief. Anything that needs to be said can, in most cases, be said in plain English. By using words and phrases he does not fully understand or by using them in the wrong context, the deceased may have said something he did not intend to say, possibly something that will cause the lawyers to rub their hands with glee as the mess is sorted out, slowly, in court. A word of warning. If you are an executor and you think this is what has happened, don't ignore it in the hope that no one will find out, on the grounds that it will cost money to go to a solicitor. If you ignore it and do the wrong thing, it can only make matters worse and take a lot longer to sort out in the long run. You may also find yourself personally liable for the consequences.

- Codicils. These are legal alterations and additions to the will, added after it was originally made and signed. To add a codicil the deceased must have gone through the same signing procedure as for the main will, though not necessarily with the same witnesses. You need to look carefully at codicils to check, first, that they are signed and witnessed correctly and, second, to ensure that they don't make a nonsense of the main will, for example, leaving the same item to two different people. There should be a statement that the will is confirmed in all other respects.

- There should be a revocation clause. This is a statement that any other will made by the deceased is now revoked (to be considered invalid). It is good practice to include this even when the deceased had not made an earlier will, just to be on the safe side. You may think that drawing up a new will automatically cancels a previous will, but it is not as simple as that. By including this revocation phrase the deceased is making absolutely sure that there will be no problems.

## ⓣ Try to Find Out If Anyone is Likely to Challenge the Will

The most loving families can be torn apart over the provisions of a will. If someone feels wrongly cheated out of something he believes is rightfully his, it is easy to imagine him shouting, 'I'm going to challenge this will in court!' But on what grounds can a will be challenged? There are two situations that are worth looking at.

### Inadequate provision made

Certain groups of people have the right to apply to the court for a share in the estate if they have been omitted from the will or where they feel they have been unfairly treated. Obviously, the aggrieved person has to have some kind of serious claim on the deceased – this does not apply where, for example, the postman feels the deceased should have left him something to make up for ten years of coping with his hostile dog. To have a valid claim, a person must be a close family member (for example, surviving spouse, children, a partner who has lived with the deceased as a spouse for at least two years, ending in death), or someone maintained by the deceased. This can include an ex-wife, where the divorce settlement did not cover this situation, and a mistress. Clearly, this is a potential hornet's nest.

### Deceased of unsound mind

The challenge would be on the grounds that the deceased was not fully aware of what he was doing and its implications when he drew up the will or that someone exerted undue influence over him. If you think you might be facing this situation, you will respond by producing medical evidence to show that this was not, in fact, the case.

If there is the threat of a serious challenge you absolutely must see a solicitor: this is not something you can handle on your own. However, remember two things. First, the person making the challenge may have got his facts wrong. He may have told you he was going to challenge the will without first speaking to his own solicitor, and so he may be in for a rude surprise. The second thing to remember is that he will certainly get a rude surprise when he sees how much it is likely to cost. The amounts of money involved have to be substantial to make it worth his while after paying lawyers' fees. Such situations are therefore unlikely to affect the average family, but it can happen. Common sense all too often goes out of the window where wills are concerned.

## Can This Will Possibly Be Problem Free?

By now you are probably wondering whether there can be such a thing as a straightforward will, one that isn't going to cost the estate a fortune in solicitors' fees. Skim quickly through the last few pages again. You'll see that many if not all of these points are simply not applicable to your situation. The average person leaves a moderate estate consisting of a family home, some savings, a car and personal effects. Provided the deceased has explained what he wants in clear and simple terms, you should have no problems.

## 🅣 Learn How to Read a Will

Now you have learned what a will should contain and what to look for, reading it should be easy. Practise on the very simple will shown on page 138. Any words or phrases you haven't already learned will be explained as you go through it.

🅗 Lawyers tend to leave punctuation, particularly commas, out of any documents they draw up. The reason for this doesn't matter: the practical effect is that at first sight it makes the document look daunting to the average person, with its endless flow of words and legal phrases. The trick is mentally to put in commas and full stops where they naturally fall. That makes the whole document much easier to read. Remember, however, that putting punctuation in the wrong place can change the sense of a sentence. If you are not entirely happy about your punctuation, or if English is not your first language, ask for help from someone who is more confident. Most people, however, should have no problems with simple wills and it really does make them much easier to read. Also, try reading the will out loud.

---

## SAMPLE WILL

This is the last will and testament of [full name] of [full address].

1.  I revoke all former wills and testamentary dispositions made by me

2.  I GIVE all my property both moveable and immoveable whatsoever and wheresoever to [full name] of [full address] ABSOLUTELY but SUBJECT to payment of all my debts funeral and testamentary expenses and appoint [him/her] sole Executor[Executrix] of this will PROVIDED ALWAYS that if [he/she] shall predecease me leaving a child or children living at my death then in lieu thereof I GIVE all my property as aforesaid to such child or children and if more than one in equal shares absolutely PROVIDED FURTHER that if all the foregoing beneficiaries shall predecease me then in lieu thereof I GIVE all my property to [person/organization] absolutely.

AS WITNESSED my hand this [date] of [month] [year].

SIGNED by the Testator[Testatrix]
in our joint presence and then by us
in the presence of the
Testator[Testatrix]

---

### Lesson one

Remember on page 136 of this book that there was a paragraph explaining that the will should include a sentence revoking all previous wills? This is what this clause is saying. Look at clause 1 of this sample will. Don't worry about the phrase 'testamentary dispositions'. All you need to know is that it means basically the same thing, but in legalese.

### Lesson two

Now look at the very bottom of the will, by the witnesses' signatures. There is a sentence starting 'Signed by the Testator/Testatrix...' This is the attestation clause, telling you that the deceased and the witnesses signed in one another's presence, and in the right order (see page 127 if you need to jog your memory).

A testator is a man making a will. A testatrix is a woman making a will. As you can see, the law hasn't quite caught up with unisex words and phrases yet.

## Lesson three

The next thing to do is to tackle that huge great mass of words which forms clause 2. As it stands, it is totally daunting. Make things easy for yourself – reduce it to bite-sized lumps.

First of all, look at the words in capital letters. Capital letters in a legal document mean that that word, or those words, are intended to stand out because they are important.

Secondly, remember that wording in legal documents cannot be ambiguous. As a result it often seems too precise and pedantic. The first two lines are a good example:

'I GIVE all my property both moveable and immoveable whatsoever and wheresoever to...ABSOLUTELY'

Now, a lot of people might just write 'I give all my property...', meaning everything they possess. In that case, what they meant isn't what they've written. What they have said is that they have given their property, but not their money or possessions. Money and possessions have to be specifically mentioned or they are excluded. This wording covers every eventuality you could possibly think of. Look again at the wording of lines one and two.

'...property moveable and immoveable...'

Well, what other kinds are there? None, of course. This wording covers the lot. But it still seems to be talking just about property. Look at the next few words.

'...whatsoever and wheresoever...'

That doesn't leave much out, does it?

In most cases, someone drawing up a will would go much further and give details of, say, the family home, by saying specifically that this property includes the house at no. 53, The Grange, New Town, or wherever. It is hard to read another meaning into all that, and that is the intention.

All the word 'absolutely' means is that they are an outright gift and not an interest for life or any other specified period (see page 130).

## Lesson four

Moving on from the words about property, look at lines:

'...subject to payment of all my debts funeral and testamentary expenses...'

When you look at that phrase without all the other words around it, the meaning is obvious – the person inheriting all the property (wheresoever and whatsoever) must pay all the deceased's debts.

## Lesson five

A great deal has already been said about executors. That is dealt with in the next phrase:

'...and appoint [him/her] sole executor/executrix...'

It is so obvious that all that needs to be said is that an executor is a man and an executrix is a woman. These days, however, 'executor' is often used to cover both men and women.

## Lesson six

If you check page 131 of this chapter you will see it explains that the person making the will must say what should happen to the money, etc if the beneficiary dies first. That is dealt with in the words:

'...PROVIDED always that if [he/she] shall predecease me leaving a child or children living at my death then in lieu thereof I GIVE all my property as aforesaid to such child or children and if more than one in equal shares absolutely...'

That looks an absolute killer, but take out the legalese (the words 'in lieu thereof' and 'as aforesaid') and see if that is better. It will make even more sense if you mentally put a comma in the last line after 'children'.

What is being said here is that if the beneficiary dies first, his/her child gets the lot, if living. If there is more than one child, each gets an equal share. Read it again and see if this makes sense to you now.

## Last lesson

The last lines, starting 'PROVIDED FURTHER', state what happens if all the people named so far – the beneficiary and his/her children, if any – die before the deceased. In that case, someone else who the deceased will name gets everything. In practical terms, this is often a charity.

## Conclusion

If you have worked through this example you will see there is nothing in the will on page 138 that you have not already read about in this chapter. What is off-putting is the lack of punctuation and the legalese. The real lesson to be learned is that when you are reading a will, take it slowly, phrase by phrase: don't try to read it straight off as you would a Jeffrey Archer novel. If you take it slowly you will be able to work out any legal phrases which are new to you, but by now, you have already met the most common ones.

The example given is of a simple will, but you can imagine that finding a few extra bequests or some extra sentences should not give rise to any problems. As long as you take it slowly you should be fine. Be aware that more complex wills can contain extensive administrative provisions which can seem alarming to the lay reader. However, take it slowly, line by line, and the sense of what you are reading should become clear. As always, if in doubt, seek professional advice.

Before finishing this chapter on wills it might be helpful to look at two situations where the legal situation is a little surprising, and which might affect the will you are now dealing with.

## ❶ Decide If Any of These Special Cases Apply

### Remarriage

Amazingly, remarriage completely invalidates an existing will, unless the will is what is called a 'mutual will' (described below). It doesn't just invalidate the clauses relating to the first husband or wife, it invalidates the whole thing. Even worse, unless the deceased made a fresh will after his new marriage, under the law he has died intestate (without leaving a will), and certain rules come into play as to what happens to his property, regardless of his wishes. (See Chapter 15 for more details on intestacy.) If you are dealing with a will you need to check whether it was made before or after the new marriage. If it was made before the new marriage make an urgent search for a later will and if you cannot find one, head straight for the nearest solicitor.

There are ways around this problem, and the deceased may have used one of these. If he has included a statement in the will to the effect that it will not be revoked on marriage, such a statement, if properly worded, is enough to prevent this problem arising. He might also have said that the will is conditional on the marriage taking place. If it did, the will stands.

### Mutual wills

A 'mutual will' is one where both parties agree that neither of them will change their will again after a specific event has taken place. To put that in rather simpler terms, George and Mary might decide to draw up mutual wills. George's will might then promise that he won't amend or revoke his will after Mary's death. Mary would make the same promise, obviously naming George as the other party.

## Co-habitees

It is quite common, especially among younger people (who might not have thought about making a will at this stage) to live together for a while without marrying. It is also legally impossible in this country at the moment for gay couples to marry. Therefore, you have the situation where a couple, genuinely committed to one another, have no legal ties. The law treats these people differently to the way it would treat them if they were married, especially where property is concerned.

The basic situation is that the deceased's estate does not automatically pass to a 'co-habitee' – if either or both partners want their possessions and property to pass to the other, they must make a specific statement to this effect in their will.

Even if this is done, there is still a problem relating to tax, if the estate is large enough for this to be payable. The law discriminates between married and unmarried partners by allowing a tax exemption on goods and property passing to a surviving spouse, but this does not apply where the two were not married.

However, the news is not entirely bad as, if the deceased hadn't made provision for the surviving partner, he/she might still be able to claim through the courts for part of the deceased's estate.

## Next step

This depends on whether an executor was named or not. If one was, and assuming it was you, Chapter 14 will explain your rights and duties. If there was no valid executor named or if there was no will at all, see Chapter 15 for what to do next.

# 14

# Executors and Probate

If the deceased named you in his will as an executor, he has made a public statement that you are capable and honest. He has entrusted the money and property he accumulated during his life into your hands. But what exactly is an executor, and what does he do?

**🅣 Make Sure You Understand What an Executor is and What He Does**

An executor is a person named by the deceased in his will and tasked with the job of managing his estate after his death.

### What is an estate?

An 'estate', when you are talking about wills, is the word used to describe the money, property and possessions the deceased left behind when he died.

### What are the duties of an executor?

If you have been named as an executor, it is not up to you to decide how much or how little work you want to do in managing (administering) the deceased's estate: the tasks you have to complete are laid down by the law. If you needed convincing that being an executor is no easy option, look closely at this list. In non-legal terms you must:

- Find out exactly what the estate consists of. This means you need to find out what the deceased owned and what debts he had. (See Chapter 16 for more details of this.)

- Discover whether any money is owing to the deceased under pension schemes or from social security benefits.

- Find out if the deceased made any substantial gifts during his lifetime, particularly in the last seven years, as this may affect the amount of inheritance tax (if any) which is payable by reason of his death.

NB
- If the deceased owned anything of considerable value, such as property, stocks and shares or antiques, get them properly valued.

NB
- Find out whether any property was in the deceased's name only or was in joint names.

NB
- Put a total value on the estate by subtracting the amount he owed in debts from what he owned.

- Make sure the funeral takes place and that it can be paid for.

- If the deceased left a business which he ran as a sole trader, continue this business in a way that keeps the goodwill (don't let it run down). Arrange, if need be, for the sale of the business.

NB
- If necessary, obtain a grant of probate.

NB
- Pay people to whom the deceased owed money and also pay debts incurred by the death itself (for example, the bill for the funeral).

- Keep within the law in administering the estate.

- Complete the administration as quickly and efficiently as possible.

NB
- Prepare accounts for the estate.

NB
- Pay all expenses incurred in administering the estate.

NB
- Pay all bequests.

NB
- Make the necessary tax returns.

Obviously, this list doesn't cover all the tasks you must undertake as this will differ from case to case, but it should give you a fair idea of what is involved. Each of the tasks listed above can, of course, be broken down into a multitude of smaller tasks, all of which must be carried out.

If you read the will carefully to see what the deceased wanted, then take an honest and common-sense approach and use the above list as a guide, you should not have any problems. Don't forget you can always bring in a solicitor or an accountant if you need specialist advice in any area. You won't be expected to pay for these yourself: their fees come out of the estate.

## Who can be an executor?

Anyone the deceased chooses. This is usually a member of the family or a close friend, but it can also be a solicitor or even a bank. There are problems if the deceased chose a minor.

## When does an executor become an executor?

As soon as the deceased dies. The executor has the authority to administer the estate from that moment. However, in practice, most executors will need to apply for 'probate' before they can do anything but the most urgent tasks (explained in more detail on page 147). Probate is a kind of confirmation that an executor does indeed have the power to manage the estate.

## Does an executor have to give his permission before being chosen?

No, he doesn't, and this can cause problems. Anyone making a will really should talk to a potential executor, explain to him how much work is likely to be involved, and ask whether he is willing to act. Most people will do this, but some don't for various reasons. It can come as a very unpleasant shock to learn that you are an executor and have just been handed a highly responsible and time-consuming task.

## ❶ Decide If You Want to be an Executor or Not

You can refuse to act, and it is quite easy to do so. Be aware, however, that you have to proceed in an official manner. You can't just stare at everyone over the top of the will after it has been read and announce that you don't want the job. Sorry – you have to do more than that. The easiest way to do this is to tell the Probate Registry and they will *NB* send you a form to fill in.

Hopefully, you won't want to consider opting out, but if you do the process of renunciation is quite simple. It is far harder to make the decision in the first place, because what you are doing is refusing one of the deceased's last requests, and an important one at that. It is not hard, however, to imagine circumstances in which you might need to consider whether you are the best person for the job, especially if you were not consulted in advance. Perhaps you have a demanding job or young family, or you are looking after an elderly relative. Don't be offended if the deceased knew this and still chose you: it doesn't mean he was ignoring or devaluing your other commitments. He might genuinely have underestimated the time needed to deal with your own affairs. Also, most people tend to downplay the extent of their problems, especially to someone who is old or infirm.

It might be that you have the time but are one of those perfectly capable people who are hopeless at administration and mentally paralysed at the sight of an official form. The deceased might not have known that, or might have thought you were joking when you talked about it.

NB

Opting out is never going to be an easy decision, but the important thing is for you to be honest with yourself. Far worse to take on the task and do a bad job. Ask yourself, first, if you want to do it and second, if you are capable of doing it well. If the answer to both is 'no', then your decision is made.

It is much harder, however, where you know you are perfectly capable of acting as executor and have the time to do so, but simply don't want to do it. One way to approach this problem might be to look at the type of person you are. Can you tackle unwanted tasks and still make a success of them, or are you the type of person who needs to feel enthusiastic about the tasks he undertakes? People are different and they deal with things in a different way. This is not a matter of one person being better than another, simply a matter of personality types. You also need to consider guilt and, perhaps, resentment. Are you going to be chewed up with guilt if you opt out? If so, perhaps taking on the task of executor might be the less painful option. And what about resentment? If you are going to seethe with resentment every time you have to stay home to write another letter instead of going to the pub or the cinema, you should consider whether this is going to work.

It is also possible that you are keen to act as an executor but you simply don't have the time at the moment. There are ways in which you can keep your options open, becoming actively involved in the administration of the estate at a later stage. It is best to see a solicitor on the details of how to go about this.

Ultimately, it is a matter of what is going to best serve the deceased's interests. He has entrusted you with managing his estate. There may be occasions when the most sensible way of ensuring matters are managed well is to hand them over to someone else. If, however, you do decide to act as executor, make sure it is a complete commitment and that you do everything required of you.

## Can an executor be a beneficiary under the will?

Yes, there is no problem if an executor receives a bequest under the will. This is quite common where the executor is a family member or close friend as, if the deceased trusted the executor enough to entrust his estate to him, he is likely to want to leave him something to remember him by, and possibly as a reward for undertaking the task.

## ❶ Learn What is Meant By Probate and Why You Might Need to Apply For It

By now, you know whether or not you intend to continue as executor and what, in general terms, your duties are going to be. The next chapter will look at some of these tasks in more detail but first of all, it is important to consider the whole issue of probate, as this is an extremely important task which you, as executor, must decide whether or not is necessary, and must implement if it is.

### What is probate?

An executor gets his power to manage the deceased's estate from the will, and has that power from the moment of death. In some cases, that might well be all you will need and you can go ahead and manage the estate on that basis. Such cases are where the estate is a 'small estate', and you may also find probate unnecessary where the family home is in the joint names of both the deceased and his spouse, although this needs looking at very carefully. (See pages 152 and 149).

However, this is the exception rather than the rule. In most cases the executor needs to acquire a legal document which confirms his authority to act. This is to reassure people with whom the executor is going to deal that he has the right to take action and accept money on the deceased's behalf.

This document is commonly known as 'probate', and that is what it will be called in the rest of this book.

### Who can apply for probate?

Only an executor, or a solicitor acting on his behalf, can apply for probate. There is another type of document required in different circumstances, for example where the deceased died without making a will, but as an executor you don't need to bother with this. For your information these situations are discussed in Chapter 15.

### What does applying for probate involve?

It involves collecting together quite a bit of information and sending it, together with a fee, to the Probate Registry. There are two different parts to the whole process:

- Filling in nine forms and sending them in.   *NB*
- Being interviewed and swearing an oath.   *NB*

## How do you apply for probate?

You contact the Personal Application section of the Probate Registries which you will find in most large towns and cities throughout England and Wales. You can either write to them or, if it is easier, go there in person.

Explain that you are an executor and wish to apply for probate. All you are doing is collecting some forms, so there is absolutely no need to produce the will, the death certificate or any personal identification.

Another way you can apply for probate is to hand the whole matter over to a solicitor and let him handle it.

## Is there a charge for applying for probate?

Yes, there is, but there is a sliding scale of charges, so if the estate is relatively small the charge is not going to be too painful. To find out more, refer to your local probate office.

### ⓣ Apply for the Forms and Make Sure You Understand What Information You Will Need

You will receive a bundle of forms which might at first sight make you wince. In fact, most of them are fairly straightforward, although you are going to have to approach various people and organizations to get the information you need. You will also receive a booklet containing a list of Probate Registries.

ⓗ      As there are a number of forms, buy a special folder and keep   N B
        them all in this. If you lose one and forget about it, your
        application for probate will be delayed.

Check to make sure you have been given all you need. This will take time. Filling in these forms is not something you are likely to be able   N B
to do in the first week after the death unless you are extremely well organized. You should have received nine assorted forms:

- An information sheet headed 'Notes for Personal Applicants'. This lists the forms which should have been included in the bundle, together with a very brief explanation of their purpose.

- Form PA1. This is the probate application form itself and it consists of four pages. It asks you the kind of questions you might expect about the deceased – when the death took place, his occupation and marital status. It then asks questions about the will and the executors, including those who don't want to act, and about various relatives of the deceased. Finally, it asks about the applicant (or applicants). It is mostly very basic information that you will know off the top of your head or which you can find out easily. There are only one or two questions that might need more thought.

First, the form asks whether there are any of the deceased's assets which are held in another name. The answer for the average person is likely to be 'no', but you need to check this out. The other potentially tricky question is about the deceased's relatives – sons and daughters, brothers and sisters, and grandparents. If the deceased is not a family member you will probably need to contact the family to get this information. Also, in some cases, the family might genuinely not know. This might occur, for example, where the deceased was an immigrant who left family in his country of origin when he came to the UK, and has since lost contact with them. In this kind of situation, contact either a solicitor or the Probate Registry for advice on how to proceed. (Also, see Chapter 11.)

- Form PA4. This is a list of the sliding scale of fees.

- Form PA5. This is a form which applies to a specific set of circumstances, namely where the deceased left a surviving spouse, but the matrimonial home is in the name of the deceased. Apart from questions about the deceased's name and date of death, all the questions relate to any claim the surviving spouse has to ownership of the house and any financial contribution he/she might have made towards its purchase.

- The next five forms deal with Inheritance Tax. This may not apply to you, but you have to fill in these forms just in case.

  – Form IH11 is an information sheet on the payment of Inheritance Tax from National Savings. Here the law has created a Catch-22 situation. If you are liable for Inheritance Tax you must pay it before you can be granted probate. However, you don't have access to the deceased's money to pay it until you have probate. (Don't you sometimes wonder who draws up our laws?) Naturally, there are ways around this difficulty and they are briefly described in this leaflet. It is worth mentioning that there are legal ways in which the amount of inheritance tax payable can be reduced, but you really need professional advice for this.

– Form IH37. This is a Schedule of Land and Interest in Land, and what is required here is simply a list of property in the estate.

– Form IHT40. This is another schedule, asking for details of all the stocks and shares the deceased owned. The average person might need to detail, for example, shares in British Gas or one of the water companies, although in some cases the list might be far longer and more complex. This is one case where it might be a good idea to get professional help as you have to give the value of these shares on a particular day. The form explains how to do it,  but you need access to a publication which might be hard  to obtain, especially if you don't live in a major town or city.

– Form IHT44. Here you are being asked to provide a complete list of all the deceased's assets and debts. This is probably the form that will be the most time-consuming to research and fill in.

– Form IHT205. This form, to a certain extent, is asking for information you have already provided on some of the other forms, but in a different way. It is all about the value of the estate and it is to see if the estate is going to attract Inheritance Tax.

### ❶ Work Out What Information You Need and How to Get It

From this list of forms you can see that it is highly unlikely that you can just sit down and fill them in off the top of your head. You are going to have to have searched through the deceased's papers and questioned people like bank managers to make sure you know exactly what the deceased owned and owed, but at least now you know what is expected of you.

 ❿ Sit and list the questions on both sides of a sheet of A4 paper. This will save you shuffling through nine different forms to see exactly what information you need.

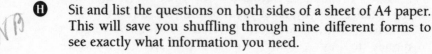

To fill in the forms correctly you are going to need to value the estate: this whole topic is discussed in detail in the next chapter. You may also find Chapter 10 'People to Tell' useful as it provides a checklist of people you might need to contact.

### ❶ Send Off the Completed Forms

Where you send them depends where you want your interview to take place. You have a choice between the larger offices and the smaller local offices, which might be more handy for you.

Don't send your forms to the local office: this would be too logical and bureaucracy doesn't work like that. Instead, look down the list of larger offices to find the one that controls the local office where you want the interview to take place. Send your form there.

❶ Keep a photocopy of the forms in a safe place. Also, make a note of the date on which you sent them.

### What happens when the forms are completed and sent off?

In the short term, not a lot. There will be a delay while the forms are being processed and there is nothing you can do to speed things up. The length of time varies according to the workload of the different offices. It is vital for you to remember that you cannot undertake any major tasks towards winding up the estate while you wait for the forms to be processed, though you can deal with minor things such as writing letters notifying people of the death.

Eventually, you will receive notification giving you the date of your interview.

### The interview and oath

The interview is to give both you and the people at the Probate Registry the chance to ask any questions and to confirm that the information on the forms is correct. As long as you have filled in the forms accurately there should be no problems.

Swearing an oath is not something you should take lightly in any circumstances, but it is nothing to be afraid of. There are certainly no judges standing around in wig and gown or bolts of lightning from on high, so if it is the first time you have had to swear an oath, don't let the thought of it put you off. If you are not religious you can 'affirm', which should not offend your conscience.

### Receiving the grant of probate

This will be sent to you through the post. Once you receive it you are free to start winding up the deceased's affairs. Most people you are about to deal with will probably need to see the document.

## Is it possible to obtain copies?

Certainly. There will be a small fee for each one, and you would be wise to obtain more than one copy, especially if the deceased held shares, as these will be needed when the shares are sold.

## ⬤ Understand What is Meant By a Small Estate

The law accepts that where an estate is very small it might well be unnecessary for you to go through this procedure. A small estate is one that consists of approximately £5000, or less, in cash, which might be deposited in a bank or building society, and where there is no property owned.

You might find, even if the estate is worth slightly more than £5000, that the bank or building societies are prepared to release the money on production of the will alone. It is worth trying this first, to save you going through the time-consuming task of obtaining probate.

Once you have obtained probate, you can start to administer the estate.

# 15

# Intestacy and Letters of Administration

If you have just discovered that the deceased failed to make a will, don't worry, you are not alone: many people in the UK die without leaving instructions about what should happen to their money and property. When this happens the person is said to have died 'intestate'. If this is the situation you are facing, there is good news and bad news. The good news is that you are not going to have to make any difficult (and possibly highly unpopular) decisions as to how the deceased's money and property is to be distributed. There is a piece of legislation dealing with the situation and it lays down in great detail how the estate is to be divided among the family he left behind. These instructions are commonly known as the 'intestacy rules'.

The bad news is that someone has to be responsible for organizing this, and for administering the estate generally. If there had been a will, the likelihood is that the deceased would have appointed someone he trusted to undertake this task. Because there is not, this person (or people – there can be more than one) has to be appointed in a different way. You cannot simply volunteer and get started on the job immediately: money and property are involved and so there is a procedure you must follow to make your appointment official. This procedure, which is not at all difficult, is known as 'applying for a grant of letters of administration', a real mouthful which sounds more off-putting than it is.

You must not take any action to administer the estate until you have received your letters of administration, as until then you have no more legal right to manage the deceased's money and property than his cat. So who can be an administrator, and exactly how do you go about obtaining this grant of letters of administration?

## ❶ Understand What is Meant By Administrators and Letters of Administration

### What is an administrator?

An administrator is a person who has the legal power to manage the deceased's affairs after his death.

### Who can become an administrator?

Basically, the surviving spouse if there is one, and anyone who has a blood relationship to the deceased, even if the relationship is quite distant. There is an order of priority in which these relatives can apply, which is:

- The surviving spouse.

- Sons or daughters (or their sons or daughters, ie the deceased's grandchildren, if the deceased's offspring died before the deceased himself).

- The parents of the deceased.

- The deceased's brothers or sisters or their children.

- Half-brothers or sisters, ie those who have one natural parent in common with the deceased.

- The deceased's grandparents.

- Uncles and aunts.

### Must someone at the top of this list become an administrator?

No. The list is about rights and not duties. What it is saying is that those closest to the deceased have the first right to apply for letters of administration, if they choose to do so. If they don't, they can renounce that right using a very simple procedure. All they have to do is to contact the Probate Registry for the correct form, in which case the next person on the list now has the first right to apply. That person in turn can renounce, right down to the most distant relatives.

## ❶ Decide Whether You Want to be an Administrator

The list makes applying for letters of administration sound like a tremendous privilege, in which those with the closest ties to the deceased having access to this privilege first. In fact, being an administrator, like being an executor, is a highly responsible and time-consuming task. It may well be that someone high on the list is horrified at the thought of administering the deceased's estate and would be only too happy for someone with a lesser claim to volunteer. Typically, the deceased's spouse may feel too stricken with grief to be able to cope with all that is involved. (See page 145 for a discussion on the right of executors to renounce or reserve their rights. The same comments apply.)

## Do relatives by marriage have a right to apply?

No. The one common thread running through the list is that, with the exception of the spouse, each possible candidate for administrator has (had) a blood relationship with the deceased. If you do not have this blood relationship you cannot apply. For example, if you are married to the deceased's sister, she can apply for letters of administration, but you cannot.

## What about partners?

If the deceased had a live-in partner, that partner cannot apply for letters of administration no matter how close and loving the relationship, or how long it has lasted unless there is a blood relationship. This may sound harsh, as it is now quite common for people to live together without marriage, but it is the law. This rule, obviously, applies to gay couples.

## What about illegitimate children?

There is no discrimination against illegitimate children. They are fully entitled to apply for letters of administration and they are included in 'children of the deceased', which means they are in the category second in line after the surviving spouse. There will, of course, have to be some proof that the applicant is a child of the deceased. This can be through some kind of legal recognition of the child by the deceased, or by a blood test. It is going to be interesting in the years to come to see how many children who are reluctantly acknowledged because of the work of the Child Support Agency take advantage of this possibility.

## What about adopted children?

They, too, are counted as 'children'. However, if they have natural parents still living – and it is now easier than it ever has been for them to trace their natural parent(s) – they cannot have it both ways and claim a right to apply for letters of administration both for their adoptive and natural parents.

## How does someone apply for letters of administration?

You can get your solicitor to apply on your behalf but you will, obviously, have to pay him to do so.

If you choose to apply yourself, the procedure is exactly the same as when an executor applies for probate: even the forms are the same. (How you do this is explained on pages 147–50.)

## What are the duties of an administrator?

These are exactly the same as those of an executor (see pages 143–4). In fact, once you have obtained the letters of administration there is no effective difference between the two.

## Does the administrator decide who gets what?

Absolutely not. If there isn't a valid will, who gets what is decided by the intestacy rules. The administrator can only make sure money and property are distributed according to these rules. There is no point in someone coming to you and saying that he remembers quite distinctly that Uncle George promised him that beautiful crystal vase on the hall table. Unless he can show he is entitled to it under the intestacy rules, all you can do is to tell him you have no power to change the law, and the law says he can't have it. (See below for details of the intestacy rules and Chapter 9 for dealing with difficult friends and relatives.)

## What are the differences between an executor and an administrator?

There are two main differences:

- An executor is appointed by the deceased through his will. An administrator is appointed by the court.

- An executor has the power to manage the deceased's estate from the moment of the death. An administrator does not become an administrator until he receives his letters of administration, and has no powers at all until then.

This second point needs some explanation. Although an executor gets his powers from the will, he usually has to obtain probate (see Chapter 14) and until he does so, there is very little he can actually do. So in practical terms, unless the estate is very small, when different rules apply, an executor and an administrator both need to go to court to get a legal document to show people in order to prove they have the right to administer the deceased's estate. The executor's document is called 'a grant of probate': the administrator's is called 'a grant of letters of administration'. The real difference is that, legally, an executor is an executor before he gets his grant and in some circumstances can act as executor, whereas the administrator has no legal standing whatsoever until he acquires letters of administration.

## Who manages the estate before the letters of administration are obtained?

Legally, no one is entitled to manage the estate before the administrators are appointed, and clearly there is a problem here as there may well be urgent tasks that need to be carried out. You should remember two things:

- You must not undertake any major tasks until you have received letters of administration.

- Urgent tasks must be taken care of.

These points seem to be contradictory but are not if you look at it with common sense. If, for example, the deceased was killed as a result of a mugging, during which his wallet and keys were taken, changing the locks on his house is clearly an urgent task which you cannot put off on the grounds that you have no power to act.

The biggest problem is likely to be money: there are things that have to be paid for but you cannot do so until you obtain letters of administration. Note that:

- Most people will understand your problem if you write to them and explain.

- In an emergency, go to the bank and try to negotiate a loan. As long as there is money in the estate this should be possible.

**H**   Make sure your bank manager knows exactly what is going on. You may not need to apply for a loan but it will save time later if you do.

## Are there any other circumstances in which an administrator can be appointed?

Yes, there are. An administrator is appointed where there are no executors. The most common reason for this is that the deceased died without leaving a will and therefore, of course, failed to name any executors. However, there are other circumstances in which there might be no executors:

- It is perfectly possible for someone to make a will but not name any executors. It is unlikely that this would happen where the will was drawn up by a solicitor: he would make sure someone was named, and if the testator couldn't think of anyone he wanted or trusted, the solicitor would suggest that he or one of his colleagues be named.

The situation is most likely to occur where the deceased drew up his own will at home. Despite the detailed instructions which come with most home-will kits, some people, inevitably, will misread them, not read them at all or simply forget the instructions as they start writing or typing.

Where this happens, the will is perfectly valid (unless the deceased has made another more crucial mistake – watch out for this), but it means an administrator has to be appointed.

- As you will now realize, it is quite possible for an executor to renounce the job. It is also easy to imagine circumstances in which an executor, or executors, are named but can't act – perhaps because they have died since the deceased drew up his will. Again, this isn't going to affect the validity of the will but someone is going to have to apply for letters of administration.

### Is the procedure the same in these cases?

In these cases, there are minor differences in procedure. When you apply for letters of administration, if a will exists, you need to send it in along with all the other forms. You will also find that the wording of the oath might be slightly different, and the list of people who can apply to be an administrator is slightly different.

### Can an administrator benefit under the will?

Of course, otherwise the intestacy rules which lay down who can apply to be an administrator would be totally unworkable. Under these rules, the people closest to the deceased are the ones who will inherit his estate. These are the same people who can apply to be an administrator. If the law did not allow administrators to inherit, it is likely there would be a distinct shortage of administrators!

### Must an administrator be appointed in every case?

No. Where the estate is small and there is no property involved, there might be no need. (See page 152 for more details of small estates.)

## ❶ Understand What is Meant By the Intestacy Rules

These are rules dictating how the deceased's estate must be distributed.

### When do the intestacy rules apply?

They apply when there is no valid will. Most commonly, that is:

- When the deceased died without leaving a will at all.
- When the deceased left a will but it is invalid for some reason.
- When the deceased married after making his will and, because of this, it has been revoked.

### Who do the rules apply to?

Anyone who dies whose main home is in England or Wales. It doesn't matter where the death actually takes place.

### How complicated are the rules?

In some cases it is crystal clear who gets what. However, it depends entirely on what the estate consisted of, how much it is worth and who survives the deceased. It can be easy to see who is to inherit, but it can also become extremely complicated.

### What are the rules?

Think of the intestacy rules as a priority list for inheritance: first the surviving spouse, then the children, then parents, then brothers and sisters, then half brothers and sisters, then grandparents, then uncles and aunts, then half uncles and aunts and then, if no one survives in any of these categories, the recipient of the estate will be the Crown, the Duchy of Lancaster or the Duchy of Cornwall.

Where the deceased leaves a spouse who survives him for at least fourteen days, the law quite rightly makes financial provision for that spouse first. It is only when money is left over that other family members will inherit.

What financial provision is made for the surviving spouse? This varies, depending on whether or not the deceased left surviving children (or grandchildren, great-grandchildren etc). Assuming, however, that the deceased had no children, then his spouse would (under the current law) receive a legacy of up to £200,000 outright (assuming, of course that the deceased left that much), plus all the deceased's personal possessions. If there is any money or property left, this is split in two: one half goes to the surviving spouse and the other half goes to the deceased's parent(s) or, if his parents are no longer alive, his brothers and sisters. If there is no one in either category, other relatives may then be entitled to share in his estate.

If the deceased left children (or grandchildren, etc), the financial provision for his spouse is slightly different to enable some money to pass to the children. Hence, the surviving spouse's legacy is reduced to a maximum of £125,000. Of any remaining property, the spouse still has a claim to half, but it is only a life interest. That means that she can receive the bank income from any lump sum (capital), but that is all. She does not receive the capital itself. The children get the other half share outright, and when the surviving spouse dies, they receive the capital in which she had a life interest.

Because of the intestacy rules, it is arguably far harder to be an administrator than an executor, and in these circumstances it may be worth spending the money to seek some initial advice from a solicitor to avoid getting in a really nasty mess.

## Co-habitees

There is one cruel and important truth. A co-habitee cannot benefit under the intestacy rules. If the deceased failed to make a will, the surviving partner must take different steps to try to obtain part of the estate by applying to the court.

Once you have obtained your letters of administration you can begin to deal with the estate.

# 16

# Valuing the Estate

The words 'value the estate' should be engraved on the heart of every executor and administrator, because this task is central to anything else you may need to do. How do you know if the deceased left enough to pay for his funeral unless you have some idea how much he was worth? How do you know you can pay all his debts unless you are sure the money is there in the first place? If you are an executor, how otherwise will you know whether you need to apply for probate?

Valuing the estate is not a hard task, at least not where the average estate is concerned, though it can be more complicated where there is, for example, property owned abroad or where the estate is large *NB* enough to attract Inheritance Tax.

What exactly is valuing the estate? It is finding out what the deceased's assets and debts are. You do it by asking people, like bank managers, who are in a position to know, and by finding any people to whom the deceased owed money. It is usually as simple as that. For the average estate, the worst you can say is that it is somewhat time-consuming and you are likely to write a lot of letters. *✗*

This chapter will discuss the type of assets and debts an executor or administrator might need to consider, and look at how they can be valued correctly.

❶ **Understand You Have a Duty to Maximize the Estate**

It is one of the legal duties an executor or administrator accepts when he takes the job that he must maximize the value of the estate. *✗* In plain English, you must get as much as you can when you sell something, must put a realistic value on, for example, a house, and must collect in all the debts you can. This is because you must act in the best interests of everyone concerned. You must make sure that there is as much money as possible to be distributed to the beneficiaries, but you must also make sure that there is enough money to pay all the deceased's debts. Therefore, you cannot, for example, sell of an item at below-market value because the purchaser is a friend and has had his eyes on it for years. This is not just a matter of personal morality – it is a legal duty, and you can find yourself in serious trouble if you don't work to place a good value on the estate.

## ❶ Set Up a Separate Account

Because you are dealing with other people's money, if you are an executor or administrator you must keep up-to-date and accurate accounts of all matters relating to the estate, and keep these quite separate from any accounts you keep of your personal finances or any business you may run. It is also going to be necessary for you to produce accounts if you need to apply for probate.

It is a good idea, in fact a virtual necessity, to open an account specifically for estate matters. This is usually done at the bank (or one of them) at which the deceased held an account and is known as an 'executor's account'.

### Claiming back expenses from the estate

Acting as executor or administrator is, to a certain extent, a labour of love. As you will already have discovered, you are not going to be paid for doing it, unless you are a professional, such as an accountant, and the will provides for you to charge your normal fees. Even if the deceased does leave you a little something in his will, this is very unlikely to be the market rate for an administrative task which might take up your spare time for weeks. Under these circumstances it would be grossly unfair to expect an executor or administrator to pay any expenses incurred while administering the estate, and the good news is that you are not expected to. All reasonable expenses relating to the administration can be reclaimed from the estate.

Clearly, there is a link here with your duty to maximize the value of the estate. You have to be sensible about these expenses. It might be quicker and more pleasant to hire a helicopter to travel to Manchester, but there are other and cheaper ways to travel, so that is what you must do.

❶ Carry a small notebook and folder with you wherever you go if you are dealing with estate business. Make an immediate note of the expense in this book and file any receipts in the folder.

## 🅣 Identify the Assets

Obviously, the assets left by the deceased will vary from estate to estate, but if we assume the deceased was an average family man who owned a car, a house and had a bit of cash in the bank, it would cover most situations. Of course, there will be some people who die and leave far greater amounts – investments in a tax haven and property scattered all over the country – but their executors and administrators are likely to be able to hand the whole matter over to a solicitor and not need a book like this to help them see what they need to do next.

Therefore, our average man who has just died is likely to have some or all of the following as assets, which are basic to the way he structured and financed his life:

- Money kept in a High Street bank, National Savings Bank or Building Society.

- A pension.

- Money owing to him from state benefits.

- A house, owned either solely by himself or jointly with his wife.

- Contents of house.

- Car.

He might also have money owing to him from a variety of other sources such as:

- The Inland Revenue (a tax rebate).

- A holiday company, for the holiday he paid for and never had a chance to take.

- A society or club membership, where the unused portion can be reclaimed.

- Health insurance premiums.

These are going to depend very much on the individual and his lifestyle.

## 🅣 Locate the Assets

So how, exactly, do you approach these people who have information about the deceased's finances and at what stage? In Chapters 10 and 11 the whole business of working out who might hold information you need and how to track them down has been discussed in some detail. The important thing is that you approach these people as soon as possible. If nothing else, you need to know if there is enough money to pay for the funeral.

## Asking for information

First of all, contact them to tell them the deceased has died, using one of the sample letters in Appendix 4 if you are too stressed at this time to think coherently. Then, either in the same letter or using one of the sample letters in the Appendix, explain who you are, what you want and why you are entitled to ask this question (ie, you are an executor or you intend to apply for letters of administration).

## People to Contact

- Banks and Building Societies. The information you are asking for is usually highly confidential and will not normally be released to anyone other than the person who opened the account. In fact, in the case of High Street banks, it is often hard enough to discover information about one's own finances – have you ever tried asking for your current account balance over the phone?

  Everyone realizes, however, the problems created by a death. As long as you produce some kind of evidence that the death has taken place – a copy of the will and/or the Death Certificate – you should receive a statement as to whether an account or accounts was held there, and the amount in the accounts. You also need to ask that this be an up-to-date figure. You may have found paying-in-books and cheque stubs, but you can't rely on these. First, there is the hole in the wall, and how many people keep flawless records of every time they use it? Second, interest might need to be calculated on the money in the account. You must have this accurate figure.

- Pensions. There are several different types of pension schemes and you need to know exactly what the position is. You may find that any pension which was being paid to the deceased ceases upon his death. You may find that a surviving spouse is entitled to a proportion of this on an on-going basis for the rest of her life. You may even find that the organization will pay out a lump sum now that the death has occurred.

If the deceased had made pension arrangements, there should be papers about this somewhere among his effects. However, perhaps there are not – people do lose things over time – or maybe you have found them and cannot make head nor tail of them.

Write to the Pensions Department of the organization for which the deceased worked, explaining exactly what the situation is. You need to write to them anyway, telling them about the death, but if you do not know the position, say so honestly. Do not feel you are in any way being foolish or inadequate: dealing with pensions is a specialized area and it will not be the first time the Pensions Department will have had to deal with letters such as yours.

If you do have papers, include photocopies of them (not the originals), and any reference number you come across. If the Pensions Department needs the originals for any purpose, you can send them later by registered mail.

- State Benefits. You need to find out first which, if any, benefits the deceased was claiming or entitled to. Make a search of his papers to see if there are any books or cheque stubs (for example, for Housing Benefit). Write to these people telling them of the death and explaining you are an executor or administrator trying to find out what the situation is. If you can't find evidence that he was claiming but suspect he was, write anyway.

Don't make unnecessary work for yourself. All the deceased's details will be on computer if he was claiming benefits. Let them check their records and then you will know exactly where you stand.

You may receive some cheques in the post for various benefits as:

- Some benefits are paid in arrears, so there may still be cheques to arrive covering a period before the deceased's death.

- There is often a gap between a department receiving news of the death and this information being logged on their computer.

In these circumstances the cheques are likely to be in the deceased's name. You cannot therefore pay them into an account, as the deceased's bank account will have been frozen when you first notified the bank (see page 164). What you should do is take a photocopy of the cheque and any enclosed letter, then return the cheque to the department explaining what has happened and giving the name of your executor's account. If the estate is entitled to this money, for example, where a benefit is paid in arrears, the department will reissue the cheque in that name. If you are the sole beneficiary and you are not going to apply for probate, explain that and ask for the cheque to be made out to you.

- Mortgage. If you have the mortgage details to hand, write to the mortgage company giving full details and ask how much is outstanding from the date of the death.

  You need to find out whether the house was owned by the deceased alone or jointly with the spouse, as this may affect the value of the estate (see page 168).

- Contents of house. Where these do not pass to the surviving spouse (see page 159), you need to put a value on the contents of the house. This value is what they would fetch if sold second-hand on the day of death.

  You can either put an estimated value on these yourself, or you can call in a firm which specializes in house clearances and valuations.

  You should know that:
  - The value of second-hand furniture is very low indeed, unless certain items are antiques. In this case, they should be valued separately by an expert.
  - Some house clearance firms are reputable and honest. Others are very dubious indeed. Be careful who you call in (see Chapter 12).

- Car. The second-hand value of a car can be given with some accuracy by a reputable garage.

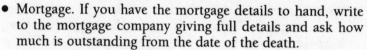

### ❶ Identify the Debts and People to Whom They Are Owed

Again, these will depend very much on the lifestyle of the deceased but most people will owe money to:

- Utilities companies (water, gas, etc).
- Credit card companies.
- Large stores on charge cards.
- Banks for an overdraft.

THIS FAR

The best way to find out exactly what is owed is to write to everyone to whom the deceased might reasonably have owed money and wait for a short time for the bills to come in.

Other debts owed might be harder to discover, such as outstanding magazine subscriptions, but as you have undoubtedly discovered in your own life, people are remarkably efficient at sending reminders when money is owed.

You must, however, not wait too long and allow things to drift. You have a duty to settle the debts and you must make an active effort to locate these people within a reasonable time.

When you have discovered who these people are, you need to explain to them that nothing can be paid until probate has been granted (assuming you are applying for probate). They will understand the situation as this will have occurred before.

If you suspect the deceased owed money to other people, but you do not know who these people are and cannot find out, there is one further thing you would be well advised to do, and that is to advertise for the creditors to come forward. If you state that they should do so within two months and they don't, they lose the right to claim on the estate. This means that you can be sure at the end of that time that no more money needs to be paid out to creditors, and this will help you put a value on the estate. It also protects you legally.

You should advertise in the local paper and also in the *London Gazette,* which is considered an official noticeboard for this kind of announcement, even though many people will not have heard of it.

## Other debts to be paid out of the estate

These are debts you will know about, because the money will be owed to you. They are the reasonable expenses incurred in the administration of the estate and the funeral expenses.

**H**    If you have set up a special account, arrange for the funeral account to be sent straight to the bank manager.

## Property

This is worth looking at separately because the situation can become a little complicated.

The first thing you must do is find out in whose name the house was held. It might have been held by the deceased alone, or jointly by the deceased and the surviving spouse (or indeed, someone else).

A house can be owned either joint tenancy or tenancy in common. You need to find out which applies in this situation. (Note that the word 'tenancy' in this context has nothing to do with paying rent.)

It is important because if it is a joint tenancy, the deceased's share of the house automatically goes to the other person, usually the surviving spouse.

In all other cases, it is wise to consult a solicitor.

## ❶ Value the Estate

When you have assessed the value of all the assets and deducted all the debts (including funeral expenses and money due to you), you can put a value on the estate. You do this by deducting the amount of the debts from the assets. This amount is what will be distributed to the beneficiaries.

## ❶ Distribute All the Bequests

You are finally in a position to distribute all the bequests the deceased made in his will.

❶    Make sure you get some acknowledgement in writing that each beneficiary has received his bequest. Keep this in a safe place.

## ❶ Understand About Inheritance Tax

This may not affect you as the value of the estate, after debts have been deducted, has to be over £200,000 to attract the tax. If you do feel the estate will be affected, see a solicitor as there are legal ways in which this tax burden may be reduced.

# 17

# Financial Problems and Solutions

In the days and weeks immediately after a death you are likely to spend much of your time dealing with finances. This is an area where you might come across some problems. Some of these are easy to solve if you know the answers, others are more difficult. This chapter will look at the sources of funds that might be available to you and some of the problems you might encounter.

## ❶ Look at Potential Problems

Each person will, of course, have his own set of circumstances to deal with, but the most common problems are likely to be:

- What to do when a widow is left with little or no money to live on.
- How to find the money to pay for the funeral.
- If you are an executor, how to identify the deceased's assets and unlock them.
- If you need to apply for letters of administration, how to solve the Catch-22 situation of obtaining access to the deceased's estate in the weeks before you actually obtain that authority from the courts.
- What you do when all bank and building society accounts are in joint names.

Each of these will be discussed in more detail below.

## ❶ Identify Possible Sources of Money

In general, the potential sources of money you should think about are:

- State benefits.

- Company pensions.
- Bank and building society accounts.
- Insurance policies.
- Bank loans.
- Loans from friends.

This last should definitely be a last resort – nothing ends a friendship more quickly than asking for a loan, but if all else fails you might need to consider it.

As you will see by looking more closely at the potential problems, one or more of these sources can be tapped in each case.

## Where a Widow is Left With Little or Nothing

### Small estates

If the deceased left you with a small amount of money but no property, ironically in the short term you are in quite a good position because you will almost certainly not have to apply for probate. You have inherited what is known as a 'small estate', and in most cases all you have to do is take a copy of the will and the death certificate and you can claim what money there is almost immediately. (See page 152 for more details of small estates).

Even if you have been left property you still have ways in which you can obtain the money to carry you over the first weeks while you sort yourself out. If the house was in joint names you might inherit automatically (see page 168) and so not need probate. Even if it was not, and you are going to have to go to the courts, you have an asset and can approach a bank manager for a loan, although of course he will need to look at the deceased's outstanding debts as well.

The comments above also, of course, apply not only to widows but to anyone inheriting a small estate (see page 152).

### State benefits

The most important thing to know is that you will not be left destitute. This prospect is something which often terrifies older people who do not know their way around the benefits system, but although it is often slow and the money you receive is hardly a fortune, remember three things:

- You are entitled to claim. This is not charity and you do not have to beg for it – you have earned it over the years by working and paying National Insurance contributions or by keeping house for the breadwinner of the family.

- If things are desperate, you can ask for an emergency payment. No one is going to allow you to go without food or be thrown out into the street, especially if you are elderly and alone.

- If you are totally bewildered by the system, you can go to your local Citizen's Advice office and they will help you.

To find out your entitlement, you should contact your local Department of Social Security: you can find the address from the phone book. It is strongly advised that you go there personally rather than phone for information. As anyone who has had dealings with the DSS will know, the offices are (generally) staffed with people who are almost unreachable by phone. This is not a slur on the DSS but is a result of the huge workload at most offices and the sheer volume of people phoning in for information. It has to be said that they are trying to improve matters at the present time, with considerable success in some areas. However, it is still better if you visit in person as you will need to collect a number of leaflets and it might be helpful to speak to one of the staff if they are available, or make an appointment to see someone. Be prepared to wait in a queue for some time.

The golden rule is – if you don't ask, you don't get. Always ask if you are eligible for any benefit which seems to apply to you. Leave it to the DSS to decide whether you come within the rules or not.

There are a number of benefits aimed specifically at widows, although there are certain rules about who is eligible and who is not. They are often lumped together under the term 'Widows' benefits', but that is slightly misleading as different benefits apply to widows in different situations. The key is the number and type of National Insurance contributions the deceased paid. You might be super-organized and know exactly what the situation is, but most people have only the vaguest idea – simply that National Insurance is something they pay regularly, or are credited with if they are on benefit ('credited with' means, effectively, that the state pays it when you can't). The DSS will have full records of the deceased's contributions and will check the situation for you.

A widow is entitled to claim the following benefits provided the deceased had paid the right number of National Insurance contributions and you were married to him at the time of the death.

Widows' Benefit does *not* apply to co-habitees.

The benefits you might be entitled to are:

- Widows' Pension. To qualify for this you must have no dependent children (there is a separate benefit if you do). This benefit is related to your age. If you are under forty-five, you are not eligible (unless you were widowed before 11 April 1988). Then, there is a sliding scale of what can be paid to you up to the age of fifty-five. After that, provided the deceased paid the right contributions, you are entitled to the full amount. If the deceased did not pay the right contributions you might still be eligible for a portion of the pension, so it is really worth applying for this.

- Widowed Mothers' Allowance. This is the benefit to apply for if you have dependent children. There are rules about what counts as 'dependent', and they are that the child (or children) must:
  – Usually be living at home.
  – Be under school-leaving age.
  – Be part of the normal family (that means you can't, for example, claim for a child of your husband's previous marriage who lives with his mother and whom you never see).
  – Be under nineteen (in some circumstances).

This benefit provides you with the amount you would get under the Widows' Pension plus an allowance for each child.

You can also claim if you are expecting the deceased's child but it has not yet been born.

- State Earnings Related Pension. You may be entitled to this if the deceased joined a contracted-out pension scheme. You need to check the deceased's papers or write to the Pensions Department of the company he worked for if you are not sure of the situation.

- Widows' Payment. This is a one-off lump sum which you may be entitled to if:
  – You are under sixty.
  – Your husband was not receiving a retirement pension.
  – He had paid the right number of contributions.
  (The good news, if you are eligible, is that this is tax-free.)

- War Widows' Pension. In certain circumstances you may be entitled to this benefit. To find out more, don't contact the

DSS because this is dealt with elsewhere: you need to write to the War Pensions Directorate (address in Appendix 5). They also have a helpline. Basically, the deceased's death must have been caused by military service or he must have already been receiving an constant attendance allowance from them.

## What forms are needed?

The good news is that you only need to fill in one form. The bad news is that is asks for quite a lot of detail.

The form you fill in is officially called Form BW1, but simply asking for the 'widows' benefit form' should get you what you need.

If you filled in and sent off the form for the DSS (Form BD8) which the Registrar gave you, you might receive this form in the post anyway, but it will certainly speed things up if you go and pick one up in person.

## How often are these benefits paid?

This is up to you. On the form you can state whether you want the money to be paid weekly, via the post office or quarterly, into a bank or building society account.

Your choice will depend on your financial situation and how good you are at managing money. If it tends to slip through your fingers it might be worth asking for the benefit to be paid weekly, otherwise you may run very short of money by the end of the quarter.

## What if you have income from another source?

You should still apply. You may find that any money you are earning will not affect the situation, although any other benefits you are receiving will be taken into account.

## Other benefits

You should also ask about:

- Income Support. The rules for when you are and are not entitled are quite complicated, but the basic story is that you can apply even when you have savings below a certain amount and you can even work for less than sixteen hours a week.

- Housing Benefit. This covers rent and Council Tax and you are entitled if your income is below a certain amount. The amount is not fixed but depends very much on the circumstances of the case. Again, you can have savings and still be eligible.

- Family Credit. This is the benefit which applies if you work over sixteen hours, still have dependent children and are on a low income. Having savings does not exclude you from this benefit.

## General comments

There are a few comments which need to be made:

- The benefits system often seems totally confusing to the man in the street. For example, are you entitled to both Widowed Mothers' Allowance and Family Credit, both of which apply to mothers with dependent children? It really is far simpler to lay the facts before the people at the DSS and let them sort it out. If they refuse you a benefit you can always appeal, and at least you will know specifically why you have been refused.

- There are other benefits available, but these will only apply to a small number of people reading this book and so have not been included.

- It has been said before but it is worth repeating: if you don't apply for a benefit, you are not going to get it. Millions of pounds of benefits are unclaimed each year because people who are entitled do not apply.

- This has also been said before and is even more important. These benefits are your right if you are on a low income. If you are elderly and not used to the idea of claiming a benefit, think of it as something you have earned over the years. It is definitely not charity.

## How to Find the Money to Pay for the Funeral

This is one of the first questions most people ask, especially if they are not particularly well off. The most important fact to remember is that one way or another, the funeral will take place and be paid for: in the last resort the local authority will bear the cost. How you approach this problem depends on your circumstances and those of the deceased's relatives.

## Where there is an estate and an executor

Provided there is money in the estate and no evidence that huge debts have to be paid on behalf of the deceased it should be easy. As you will know by now, in many cases an executor will have to apply for probate and the deceased's money will be frozen till then. A chat with a bank manager should sort this out. If there are assets, particularly property, you should be able to negotiate a loan.

## Where there is an estate and letters of administration are needed

This might cause more of a problem because until the letters of administration are granted, no one is legally in charge of the deceased's affairs. However, again, the thing to do is to approach a bank manager. The person to apply is someone who will inherit under the terms of that will.

If there is no will, the intestacy rules apply and it will be clear who the main beneficiary is. He can apply for a loan on that basis.

Obviously, a family member can pay out of his own money or arrange a loan on his own account. Failing this, you might be eligible to apply for money from the Social Fund (see below).

## Where there is no money

In these circumstances you can do one of three things:

- You can approach a funeral director and see if he offers a scheme which will enable you to pay over a period of months: some do but by no means all.

- Apply to the DSS Social Fund. Unfortunately the rules are rather strict. The person applying – not the deceased – must be receiving Income Support, Family Credit, Housing Benefit or Disability Working Allowance. You should also note that this is a loan and not a grant – you have to pay the money back from the estate if there is one. The funeral is, however, a proper funeral, arranged through a local funeral director.

- Apply to the local authority. Some run an inexpensive funeral scheme and you may be eligible for this.

If no one can be found who can pay for the funeral, the local authority will organize one, but the criteria for this are, again, quite strict. However, the bottom line is that no one is going to allow the deceased to remain in the hospital morgue or in his bedroom without being buried, if only for public health reasons. If you really don't know where to turn, approach some of the local funeral directors for advice: even if they can't handle the funeral they will almost certainly point you towards help. Alternatively, speak to a minister of religion: he might be able to help or to negotiate on your behalf.

## How an executor can unlock the deceased's assets

This has already been discussed in Chapters 14 and 16. If it is a small estate there is no problem, and if probate must be applied for and money is needed for urgent tasks, a bank manager is the best person to approach.

## How to unlock the estate without letters of administration

This is difficult. At least when there is an executor the banks have a named person with legal rights and duties to deal with. The best course of action is to arrange for the person likely to inherit, either under the will or under the intestacy rules, to speak to a bank manager. The good thing is that this is not an uncommon situation and provided there are assets in the estate and no large debts, people are inclined to be sympathetic to your plight.

## When accounts are in joint names

It is simple: there is no problem. The surviving person can usually gain access to the account on production of the Death Certificate. You shouldn't even need probate for this (though of course you might for other reasons).

Hopefully, you have now found a way to support yourself financially while you are discovering exactly what assets the deceased left. It is unfortunate that this should be a problem at a time when you are grieving, as it is in so many cases, but one way or another, you should find the money you need at this difficult time.

# Part
# IV

# *Special Circumstances*

# 18

# The Death of a Child

This is surely one of the most tragic deaths to have to cope with. Nothing can ease the pain of the parent or parents involved, but you can be sure that all the people and organizations you'll need to contact – funeral directors, churches and crematoria – have special rules which apply in these circumstances and try to make the days after the death as trouble-free as possible.

## Cot Deaths

The days are fortunately past when the death of a small baby in its cot or pram would be viewed with suspicion by the authorities. It was not only the police and social workers who questioned what had happened: the grieving parents were left asking themselves if there was something they had done wrong, or not done that they should have done. They had to handle not only their grief, but also a heavy burden of guilt.

Now there is more understanding of the phenomenon. This isn't going to lessen the pain felt by the parents, but it does mean they will be treated with sympathy and understanding by everyone involved. It also means that when they ask why it happened, there are support organizations, like the Foundation for the Study of Infant Deaths, set up to help them find the answers (in Appendix 5).

### What happens if there is a cot death

The certification and registration are exactly the same as for an adult. You must, however, be prepared for the fact that the coroner will be called in. If he recognizes it as a cot death, his enquiries will usually be over in a very short period of time.

## Accidents

Children are inquisitive and adventurous. They will open bottles they have been forbidden to touch and freewheel down hills on their mountain bikes. Inevitably there are accidents, and sometimes these are fatal.

179

Always phone for a doctor or an ambulance. While the child is being examined, try to contact the child's other parent: he or she will need to know, and you need some emotional support. If this is not possible or desirable for some reason, phone a friend to come and be with you.

Ask the doctor if there is a local support group, or if you are in the hospital, ask if there is a counsellor you can speak to. It is very likely you will start to think that if only you hadn't put the bottle on that shelf, or given him the mountain bike, he would still be alive. You need to speak to someone before these feelings start to destroy you.

## Illness

Watching a child fade away from life makes one feel utterly helpless. The illness may be long-standing, in which case the doctor will have prepared you for the death, or it may have been sudden in its onset, in which case you might not have had time to adjust to the fact that the child was ill, let alone dead.

It might help to learn more about the illness which caused the death, and what is being done to make sure other children don't die of this in the future. There are specialist groups for the relatives of those who have died of certain illnesses (the hospital will give you the names) and you might find it beneficial to speak to someone who has been through what you yourself are experiencing now. Many people find relief from their pain by fund-raising for these groups.

## Death in Hospital – Live birth

If at all possible the hospital will ensure the parent(s) are present at the moment of death. If it is clear the child will die, the parent(s) will often be allowed to hold the child as it passes away. Almost all hospitals will give the parent(s) time with the child after death.

## Death in hospital – Stillbirth

The days are long gone, thankfully, when a stillborn child was whisked away, never to be seen by the parent(s). If you ask to see the child and hold it, this request will almost always be honoured unless there is a specific and stated reason why not. A child born dead is as much a person as one born alive, and this is reflected in the treatment of both the infant and the parent(s).

## Bureaucracy

Certification and registration must still take place. The main difference where the child was born live is that he or she will be registered as 'son of' or 'daughter of'. Apart from that, proceed as explained in Chapter 3. The exception to this is where there was a stillbirth. In this case, the stage of the pregnancy at which the child was born dead is important. If a child is born dead before the twenty-fourth week it is considered a foetus, and the mother has legally had a miscarriage and not a stillbirth. If it is born after the twenty-fourth week the child is legally considered to have been born dead.

The first thing to note is that you must register a stillbirth at your local Registry. Who can legally do this? A wide range of people. Firstly, of course, the mother has the legal right to register the death, as does the father if the child would have been legitimate had it lived. In addition, certain people not related to the child can carry out the registration – the occupier of the house where the birth occurred, any person present at the birth, and anyone who found the dead child.

What information and documents do you need to register a stillbirth? You will need the following. The procedure is slightly different depending on whether a doctor or midwife was present at the birth or not.

If a doctor or midwife was present you will be given:

- A medical certificate signed by any doctor or midwife in attendance at the birth.

- A notice to informant, given to you by the doctor, telling you who can register the death and the kind of information you must supply.

All you have to do is to make sure the doctor or midwife gives you these forms. You will almost certainly not have to remind them: they will know the procedure.

Where no doctor or midwife was present at the birth you, or another person who was involved, have a more active role to play. You must obtain, from the Registrar of Births and Deaths, Form 35, a form which is used to make a declaration that to the best of their knowledge the birth was a stillbirth. Either of the parents can make this declaration, as can any qualified informant.

Whichever forms you acquire, you need to take them to the Registrar of Births and Deaths within forty-two days of the birth.

What happens when you go to register a stillbirth?

- Hand over the certificate signed by the doctor or midwife (or the declaration on Form 35).

- The Registrar will then ask some questions:
  - The name of the child (if it hasn't been named, say so).
  - The mother's first name, present surname and surname before her marriage (if applicable).
  - Place of birth.
  - Place of residence at the time of the birth.

- What happens next depends on whether the parents were married or not. If they are, the Registrar will want to know:

  - The date of the marriage.
  - The total number of previous children, stillborn or not, by whatever father. (This information is 'extra' information. It does not go on the register but is collected to help with government statistics to do with population trends.)

In the case of a stillbirth you will not receive a Death Certificate.

Once you have registered the stillbirth in this manner you are free to set a date for the funeral or cremation.

## The Funeral

### Cost

Most funeral directors will offer their services free of charge. This is a fact worth knowing, especially if money is tight. It is an unpleasant reality that a funeral can be expensive and the last thing you need to worry about at the moment is money. What they offer is likely to be a basic funeral. If you want extras it is reasonable that you should pay for these. However, remember that they can only waive their own charges, for things like use of the chapel of rest and provision of a coffin: there may still be small fees payable to others involved, such as the priest or vicar's fee, and a fee to the organist at a church service. It is worth asking the funeral director whether these people too will waive their fee if you are in financial distress. If you are able to afford a funeral, however, please do pay for it. If funeral directors feel they are being taken advantage of, it is possible that this good-hearted gesture might be withdrawn in the future, causing considerable suffering to bereaved families.

Most crematoria will cremate a child under one year for nothing.

### Personalizing the funeral

There are many ways you can personalize the funeral to reflect the fact that a child has died. If you are holding a religious service you can chose hymns and texts which are appropriate to a child. If you are not a regular churchgoer yourself, ask the minister to advise you.

If you can afford it you can buy a white coffin, perhaps lined with white satin. You will certainly be able to place favourite toys in the coffin to be buried with the child, or other items which would bring comfort to the child in life, such as a photo of the parent(s). The funeral director would look favourably perhaps on dressing the child in a favourite football strip or party dress.

You can also arrange with a local florist to have a flower arrangement designed in a way that has particular meaning. Some favourite options are having the child's name spelt out in flowers, or a teddy bear created out of marigolds.

Don't forget – you can also take a lock of the child's hair or take a hand or footprint, to be cast later in plaster of Paris or metal. One other thing you might want to consider. Many people these days own camcorders, which can also be hired for surprisingly little for a day or a weekend. Why not consider recording at least part of the funeral, so that there is a record of the child's last moments?

Whatever you decide to do, all involved will encourage you to design a funeral which is appropriate for the child. He or she was an individual, however short a time they lived, and has a right to have this fact reflected in their last moments.

## The burial

The fee for burying the child in a churchyard or local authority cemetery is payable to the owners of the cemetery and is one fee the funeral director cannot waive. However, you may well find that where it is a child being buried, this fee also is waived. This is more likely if the child is under one year old but some cemeteries will bury any child free of charge. Ask the funeral director to check.

## Memorials

You will have to pay if you want to erect a headstone, both for the headstone itself and for it to be installed at the grave. Headstones cannot be placed immediately after a grave has been dug as the ground must be allowed to settle, therefore if you can afford to order a headstone, you will have several months in which to consider different designs. Be sure to talk to the owners of the cemetery or churchyard as there may be restrictions on the size, design or wording of the headstone. Once you have found out what is permitted, you can commission a tribute to the child which will last for centuries. (Some suggestions are given in Appendix 3.)

Another way to celebrate the life of your child, if you can afford it, is to commission something in the child's name – perhaps a swing at the local school, or a sum of money towards the funeral expenses of another, poorer family enabling them to have more than a basic funeral.

Whatever the cause of death, it is often very useful to reach out to a support organization. (Some names and addresses are given in Appendix 5.)

# 19

# Retention of the Body by the State

In the vast majority of cases where the coroner has been called in following a death, the body will be released for burial either after a short investigation or after the post-mortem reveals the cause of death. Sometimes, however, even when his investigations are complete, the coroner will not release the body immediately, but will call for an inquest. He must by law do this whenever the death was unnatural or violent, or the cause of death unclear. You have no power to prevent an inquest taking place if the coroner believes it is necessary.

## ❶ Understand What is Meant by an Inquest

An inquest is an investigation into the death and all circumstances surrounding it. It is held so that a definite decision can be made as to the cause of death, and it takes place in a coroner's court. A coroner's court is basically a normal court of law with less rigid rules and none of the old-fashioned etiquette (wigs, gowns etc.). The person who presides is the coroner, and it is his job to make sure that everyone present obeys the court rules, to request anyone with relevant information to attend, and to question them where necessary.

## ❶ Attend an Inquest if You Are Called

Because of all his previous investigations, and those of the police, the coroner will know who he wants to attend. If he summons you, you are legally obliged to go and there are penalties he can impose if you do not. If you are called, you will be told the date on which the inquest opens: this is often done quite informally – it may even be by a phone call.

You can claim travelling expenses and money to compensate for loss of earnings, though this is not a fortune.

If you really can't go on that day, make sure you phone the coroner's office and tell them.

185

## ❶ Volunteer Any Relevant Information You May Have

If you have not been called and you have information the court should know about, you have a legal duty to volunteer this information. To do this, contact the coroner's court, tell them who you are and what it is all about.

You might be on a list of people called to attend and will thus be told the date on which the inquest starts. However, if you are not and you feel you have something to contribute, or you are just interested, perhaps because you knew and valued the deceased, phone the coroner's court or ask at the police station and they will give you the information.

### The date of the inquest

The date will not be set until the coroner is satisfied that any tests or investigations he has asked for have been completed. This can be a relatively short period of time: it can be a matter of months. It depends entirely on the coroner's judgement as to what evidence needs to be collected and how complicated the case is.

### Adjournment of inquest

If it looks as if any tests or investigations are going to take a long time, the coroner can open the inquest and then adjourn it (put it on hold) for a specific number of days, or even indefinitely. This can sometimes make it possible for you to bury the deceased before the inquest is over (see below).

## ❶ Be Prepared for What Happens at an Inquest

You have probably seen courtroom dramas on TV, with the judge and the lawyers in wigs and gowns. An inquest is not like that. For a start, there may not be any lawyers. Anyone is perfectly entitled to hire one, but it is not obligatory (nor can you get legal aid for doing so). If there are lawyers present, they will be dressed in their normal clothes, as will the coroner himself.

The coroner will call each witness to the stand in turn and question them under oath. After that, anyone 'with a proper interest' is also free to ask questions – they do not have to do so through a lawyer. People with a 'proper interest' are:

- Parents, spouse and children of the deceased.

- Any person whose conduct is called into question regarding the death.

- Insurers of the deceased.

- Beneficiaries of any insurance policy on the deceased.

- Any relevant official.

## The purpose of an inquest

One of the most important things to know about an inquest is that it is not adversarial. What does this mean? Well, in a normal court there are two sides – the prosecution and the defence. It is not their job to find the truth of what happened, but to present their side's case as well and as convincingly as possible, which is a rather different thing. They are adversaries, fighting to win.

The purpose of an inquest, however, is to get at the truth. Because of this, there cannot just be two sides. Many people may each hold one clue as to what happened, and the aim is to put all these pieces together.

## The kind of evidence presented at an inquest

A very broad range of evidence can be presented at an inquest. This is not limited to purely medical matters but can include factors such as conditions at work (where there is a possibility that the deceased died of an industrial illness or accident) or the deceased's state of mind (where there is the possibility of suicide).

## Jury cases

You may find there is a jury, although this is not common. A jury has to be called in cases:

- Where there has been an industrial accident.

- Where the death occurred in police custody or was caused by a police officer.

- Where the circumstances of the death present a danger to the public.

## The verdict

After the last witness has been questioned by anyone who wishes to do so, the end of the proceedings comes surprisingly quickly. Unlike a normal court of law there are no long speeches by lawyers summarizing their case and trying to knock down the opposition's case as there are no positions to defend. Instead, the coroner will sum up the evidence, perhaps retire to consider matters, and then deliver his verdict.

There is a wider range of possible verdicts than in a 'normal' court of law, where one can be guilty or not guilty. The most common ones are:

- Natural causes.

- Killed unlawfully/lawfully.

- Industrial disease.

- Suicide.

- Accident or misadventure.

- Industrial accident.

- Open verdict.

It is not the coroner's job to judge criminal or civil liability: this is quite a different issue and is dealt with in separate courts where necessary.

You may find in certain circumstances that the coroner adds a comment to his verdict.

## ❶ Deal with the Bureaucracy

You still need to have the death registered, but you may find the procedure is slightly different:

- Just because an inquest has been called for does not necessarily mean that it will be months and months before you can bury or cremate the deceased. The system is not entirely heartless. Where there is no doubt as to the actual cause of death or to the identification of the deceased, the inquest can open, issue the order for burial or cremation, and then adjourn until a specific date. This might happen where no one disputes the cause of death, for example, asbestosis, but the circumstances surrounding the death need to be investigated – whether the deceased worked with asbestos.

- If the body was not released until the end of the inquest, the coroner will sign the appropriate form and send it directly to the Registrar. The good news is that this form contains all the information you would normally have to provide to the Registrar in person. This means you only need visit the Registrar if you want a copy of the Death Certificate, and not for any other purpose.

Depending on the verdict of the inquest, your ordeal may not yet be over as civil or criminal proceedings can still be brought. However, you will at least be able to bury or cremate the deceased.

# 20

# Burial Without Ceremony

As we move towards the end of the twentieth century, it is possible to see how much attitudes have changed over the last hundred years. At the beginning of the century, near-destitute workers would spend their last penny, literally, in order to give a deceased family member a good funeral. They would buy the best coffin they could afford, try to provide food and drink for mourners and, of course, there would be a service in church presided over by a minister of religion. They were not alone in their attitudes. At every level in society the provision of a 'suitable' funeral was considered a must, and 'suitable' meant that money would be spent on it in accordance with the deceased's status in life. Failure to provide this often meant relatives were described as mean and uncaring.

Today, a small but increasing number of people are challenging this, for a number of different reasons. Some argue on conservation grounds that valuable resources are being wasted in opting for a traditional funeral, for example, by giving the coffin metal handles. Others believe we should rediscover old traditions, whereby the deceased was laid out, cared for and buried by family and friends. This, they argue, is an act of love and ideally should not be offloaded on to a stranger, however competent. Giving the family and friends the chance to perform that most personal of tasks is comforting, they believe, both for those alive, knowing that they will not be handed over to strangers when their time comes, and to those close to the deceased in that they are intimately involved in his last moments, not distanced from them. They argue that death is natural and it is harmful to try to hide death and its aftermath away, to distance oneself from death by physically removing the deceased and allowing strangers to make his burial arrangements.

This point of view has a great deal to commend it, but also a definite downside. In favour, one could say – as indeed this book has argued – that friends and relatives of the deceased should become as involved as possible in the design of a funeral. Distancing oneself from the event simply makes it harder to come to terms with it.

However, it is a fact that many, perhaps most, people at the present time are emotionally and practically quite unable to face laying out a member of their family, let alone building a coffin for them or knowing how to hire a hearse.

The good news is that for those who have thought about this issue and decided, after discussing it with their friends and relations, that when they die they want all necessary tasks handled by them, that it is both possible and legal. If doing things this way brings comfort to all involved, it is hard to see what objections there could be.

There are a number of practical matters which need to be thought through. This really should be done in advance of a death to give those concerned time to work out where to buy a coffin or how to build one, where to bury the deceased, where to store the body, and many other similar tasks. Therefore, if you are reading this immediately after a death, it is probably too late for it to be a viable option for you in this case. However, this chapter will discuss how to go about doing what is necessary for the deceased up to and including burial to enable you to consider whether perhaps this is an option that might appeal to you and to other members of your family in the future.

## ❶ Get Your Thoughts Straight – Decide Why You Like the Idea of a Home-Organized Funeral

Most arguments boil down to the fact that it is natural and loving. It is caring hands that will wash down the body and lay it out. The deceased can remain at home in the midst of his family prior to the burial. The last resting place will be dug by those who were with the deceased in life, and any service will be designed by them.

## ❶ Lay Out the Body

This varies according to the situation, the wishes of the deceased and the wishes of those left behind.

### Laying out and preparing the body

You need to be absolutely sure you can cope with this task emotionally before you commit yourself to doing it.

- You have to decide whether you can touch the body at all. Some people cannot stomach the idea. There is no blame attached to this: everyone has his own tolerance level in different circumstances.

- You must be prepared to do some very personal things to that body. The nightmare scenario is one in which a family member agrees to lay out his loved one, starts the task, then finds he is repelled by it. It is easy to imagine the burden of guilt that person will carry for the rest of his life. This is definitely not a task for anyone who is squeamish about the human body and its functions. However, laying out is a job which is not difficult and does not require specialist medical knowledge.

Laying out the body is the preparation of the body for death. It should be done after the doctor has certified the cause of death and when you are sure the coroner is not going to be called in.

There are only a few tasks and these are:

- It is not essential but it is customary for aesthetic reasons and reasons of respect, to close the deceased's eyes. You can do this with the palm of your hand, your fingers or with coins.

- Ensure that the jaws remain closed. The easiest way to do this is by taking a piece of cloth, slipping it under the chin, then taking each end to the top of the head, where you tie them together.

- The next task is optional but is often carried out. The body has orifices such as the nose and anus which can continue to leak fluids. These can be plugged with cotton wool.

  You must, absolutely *must*, wear disposable rubber gloves for this task, not only as a barrier to infection generally but also for a reason that most people will reject as applying to a member of their family – AIDS. This is a disease about which the medical profession still knows relatively little. It seems to be generally agreed that it is quite hard to catch unless you carry out a high-risk activity. One of these is the exchange of body fluids, through sex or, possibly, by other means. Until the truth is known beyond all doubt, it is a very bad idea to be in contact with body fluids from another human being unless you are 100 per cent sure there is no danger. You should wear disposable rubber gloves to close the orifices in any case, but while there is even the remotest chance that your fingers might touch body fluids which can enter your bloodstream through cuts, take precautions! If you feel this is an act of distrust or disrespect to the deceased, remember he or she would probably be the first to tell you to do what the medical profession do, and wear gloves.

The same applies to any open wounds on the body, such as bed sores or ulcers. Wearing gloves, make sure they are covered with a dressing.

Most people find this the task which is potentially the most distasteful, although it is a procedure that takes only a few seconds to carry out. Anyone who has ever had to look after a small child, however, should have no problems with these physical tasks.

- Empty the bladder. You do this by pressing gently on the lower abdomen. Put a towel underneath to absorb the liquid.

After the laying out you can wash the body gently, brush the deceased's hair and, if it is a man, shave him if necessary: it is a little known fact that hair continues to grow for a while after death. It is at this stage that you dress the deceased in whatever clothes you, and perhaps he, have chosen for the interment.

## ❶ Be Prepared for the Body to Change Physically

### Discoloration of the body

Gravity will cause the blood in the deceased's body to move to its lowest parts which, if the deceased is lying in bed, will be the back, buttocks and the backs of the legs. To someone caring for the deceased it will look as if these parts of the body are covered in severe bruises. This effect will appear about half an hour after death. Don't worry, as this is perfectly natural.

### Stiffening of the body

Most people, because of TV, the cinema and crime novels, will be familiar with the term 'rigor mortis', the stiffening of the body after death. The time this stiffening starts depends on several factors such as room temperature and the age of the deceased. In usual circumstances you can expect to see it appear about six hours after the death so you should try to carry out the laying out by then. The stiffening will increase for about twenty-four hours and then decline.

## ❶ Decide Where the Body is to Rest Before the Funeral

You must be careful because the body will start to deteriorate if it is not kept cool. You can:

- Ask a local funeral home if the deceased can be placed in their cold room (you will, of course, have to pay for this).

- Keep the body at home in a cool room. You cannot, however, allow too much time to elapse before the funeral takes place if you do this.

Note that there is no legal requirement for you to embalm a body unless you are transporting it.

## ◯ Obtain a Coffin

You must provide a coffin. Making one is not a particularly difficult task if you are good with your hands, but there are certain things to bear in mind.

- The coffin must be large enough to accommodate the deceased but not too large so that he moves around inside.

- It must be sturdy enough to stand up to handling, including being loaded into whatever transport you select. In particular, you should ensure that the joints are sound and the wood is sufficiently strong to prevent splintering or cracking.

- You should take some care with the exterior surfaces to prevent scratches and more serious injuries to people handling it.

- It is going to be extremely difficult to handle the coffin unless you put handles on it. These must be strong and easy to use.

- If you are planning to cremate the deceased, make sure you are not going to use anything in its construction – wood, glues, lining, metals – which is unacceptable to the crematorium. Check with them for detailed requirements.

- If you are intending to bury the deceased, make sure the dimensions of the coffin and any material used in its construction are acceptable to the churchyard or cemetery.

If you do not think you can or want to make a coffin, you could consider approaching a local carpenter, to whom such a task would be easy. What this would cost depends entirely on whom you ask and, to a certain extent, where you live.

In theory it is possible to buy ready-made coffins, either from a funeral director or from a supplier. Funeral directors, however, tend to be highly unenthusiastic about this and suppliers even less so. If all else fails, it is worth a try.

## The trimmings

Don't forget you need to line the coffin and provide some kind of name plate. Your choice of lining is the least of your problems, although do liaise with the crematorium for forbidden substances if you are planning to cremate the deceased. A metal name plate can easily be ordered and engraved via a metalworker located through Yellow Pages and should cost relatively little.

## ⓣ Don't Forget to Register the Death

Remember that the legal requirements for certification and registration are exactly the same as for any other death.

## ⓣ Arrange to Transport the Deceased to His Burial Place

You must somehow arrange to transport the deceased to the location at which he is to be buried. You are not going to be able to fit a coffin into the back of the average family car – think of the trouble you have with large suitcases and parcels. However, a hatchback might be suitable (be sure to measure it to be absolutely certain) and a small van would be ideal. If you don't own a van, think about hiring one from a company advertising in the Yellow Pages. You might also consider approaching a funeral director to see if you can hire their hearse for a morning or afternoon but you will be quite lucky to find one who is agreeable to this, and you have the additional problem of co-ordinating the time of the burial with their schedule.

## ⓣ Make Sure the Burial Authority Will Accept a Home-Organized Funeral

You should check at a very early stage whether the local churchyard or cemetery will allow you to bury the deceased there in a home-made coffin. It is hard to see why there should be objections, provided the coffin is the right size and sturdy, but it is a fact of life that some cemeteries and churchyards are not keen to encourage this.

## Gravediggers

If you are lucky enough to be granted permission to bury the deceased in a churchyard or cemetery, don't forget to organize the gravediggers.

## Burial on private land

It is theoretically possible to bury the deceased on your own land, but this is not a task which should be entered lightly, or at a late stage, as there are many issues to consider, including the question of whether or not you need planning permission, what happens to the grave if you move house and public health considerations.

## ❶ Know What the Problems Are if You Are Considering Cremation

Crematoria generally are far more strict about the materials which can be used in the construction of coffins, so you need to check first, whether they will accept a home-made coffin and second, what their requirements and limitations are.

## ❶ Design a Service or Ceremony

### Church services

Whether you will be allowed to bring the deceased into a church for a service depends almost entirely on the individual minister of religion, as this is still, to a large extent, unknown territory. Check first to see what the situation is. Where it is not permitted, you could opt instead for a service at the graveside.

### Religious service at home

There is nothing to stop you organizing a private service at home either prior to the church service or instead of it. You might be able to persuade a minister of religion to officiate, though this will depend to a large extent on his personal views on the subject of home funerals and possibly also on the extent to which he is prepared to stretch rules to do so. You are likely to have more success in asking the minister to attend in an unofficial capacity or as a friend, and perhaps bless the coffin or say a few prayers rather than hold a full service. If you cannot find a minister to do this, there is nothing to stop you organizing a prayer session of friends and relatives around the coffin.

### Non-religious services

One option you might like to consider is a non-religious service. You can do this at home, but many crematoria will allow such a service in their chapel. This can be one you design yourself or you can approach the British Humanist Association for advice and/or a service leader (address in Appendix 5).

Ⓗ  At all stages of the process, ask whichever organization and official you are dealing with whether you need to fill in any forms. The situation at the moment (1996) is as described above, but as the frequency of home-organized funerals increases the government or local authorities may intervene and require more bureaucracy.

Ⓗ  Ensure that there are several people prepared to arrange a home-organized funeral. If there are only two and someone opts out, the remaining person will be left with an unpalatable choice – approach a funeral director, or attempt the task themselves, possibly without the required skills, the right emotional approach or even the enthusiasm.

Anyone thinking about a home-organized funeral should research the subject thoroughly before making a decision. The Natural Death Centre (address in Appendix 5) should be able to answer all your questions (they also produce an information pack which you can send for, but please enclose six first-class stamps as they have few funds). There is also an excellent book on the market, *The Natural Death Handbook,* published by Virgin Books, which is available at most bookshops and which includes many names and addresses of useful organizations.

# 21

# Suicide

Suicide was a crime in this country until 1961. That is no longer the case. This means that the only investigation into a suicide will be by the coroner: there will be no police involvement at all. In practical terms, a suicide is treated exactly the same as any other death. The emotional damage done to those left behind, however, is another story.

## ➊ If Someone Commits Suicide, Phone the Doctor

If you are absolutely sure suicide was the cause of death, call the doctor, day or night. There is no need to contact the police. Sit and wait for him to come, and accept that you, and probably anyone else there, will almost certainly be in a state of shock. When the doctor comes he will examine the body, but will not give you a medical certificate (see Chapter 3). He might also prescribe a mild tranquillizer for anyone present, especially the person who found the body.

You must keep any suicide note as the coroner has to be involved in such cases.

## ➊ Accept That the Coroner Must Be Called In

A suicide falls into one of those categories where the coroner must be called in (see Chapter 3).

Show him the suicide note if there is one, even if the contents are extremely private or painful. This will make the investigation go far more smoothly, and possibly stave off further investigations.

Explain any surrounding circumstances, such as marital or financial pressures. Show him any evidence you may have of this, such as the deceased's bank statements.

If the coroner decides it was unquestionably suicide, there will automatically be a post-mortem and inquest.

If there are any doubts as to what happened, the police may be called in. This is not because suicide itself is a crime, which it isn't, but because it may, conceivably, have been murder or manslaughter. In any event, there will be a post-mortem and an inquest (see Chapter 19). There is nothing you can do to stop this process.

## ❶ How Do You Register the Death?

You don't, because of the need for the post-mortem and inquest.

## ❶ Arrange a Burial

Some people still believe that there are restrictions on where you can bury the victim of a suicide. This is no longer true: suicide victims are seen as exactly that – victims of depression and despair. They are no longer the subject of discrimination by being buried in unconsecrated ground.

Choose the burial site exactly as you would in other circumstances (see Chapter 5).

## ❶ Reach Out For Help

As you can see, the procedures are the same as for any death where the coroner is involved. This is not the problem. The problem is for those left behind to cope emotionally. There are several organizations devoted to helping friends and relatives of a suicide, such as Cruse (address in Appendix 5) and you really should think about contacting one of them. They can provide counselling and possibly a contact who has himself been through what you are now suffering.

Make sure you stay in contact with your GP: you may well need medication to help you for a while.

If you are at all religious, ask your minister for help and prayers.

# 22

# Donation and Transplantation of Organs

At any one time in this country the lives of about 5,000 people depend on their receiving an organ transplant. Some of these people will die quite unnecessarily because a donor could not be found in time. Thanks to constant publicity an increasing number of people are aware of this, and are willing to use their own death, or the death of loved ones, to help those in need. But what organs can be transplanted, and what exactly is the procedure? Is it too late by the time the will is read to discover that this is what the deceased wanted, or can medical science still benefit from the death? And what about the age of the donor – is this an important factor, or is it irrelevant?

❶ **Decide Whether to Honour the Wish of the Deceased to Donate Organs**

You will probably have heard of the donor card system. You might even carry one. These cards are immensely useful to hospitals as they show the deceased's wishes in this matter. On the surface, there should be no problem – the donor card carrier has made his views known and you have written evidence of this. It seems you have no decision to make. In practice, things are not as simple as this. Even if someone carries a donor card, most hospitals will take the views of the deceased's relatives into account and will not remove the organs if they refuse permission. Some thirty per cent of relatives do refuse permission. It is your right, but do you want to go against the deceased's wishes?

It is a good idea to talk this over with other relatives, especially if you yourself are unhappy about the idea. You can also discuss it with a member of the hospital staff, the transplant co-ordinator or the chaplain.

❶ **Know What Your Religion Says About Transplantation**

Most of the major religions permit the transplantation of organs in order to save the life of another human being, and indeed are actively in favour of it. There are some problems in the case of Muslims and Hindus, but these are practical rather than being based upon any religious objection. Both these faiths have fairly strict procedures to follow after a death – speed of burial and the fact that the body must not be handled by a non-believer – but there is no actual prohibition against removing organs for transplant.

If you are a member of one of these faiths, wish to sanction the removal of organs but obviously don't want to go against procedure, explain this to the hospital and they might be able to come up with an arrangement that will satisfy everyone.

The only groups which will not sanction transplantation are Christian Scientists, certain Orthodox Jews and some of the smaller Protestant movements.

If you need reassurance on this, call your minister of religion and ask for his views. Doing this in advance of a tragedy might save the lives of a number of people you may never meet.

## T Act Quickly

If you want to sanction organ donation from the deceased, be aware that time is a critical factor. You cannot wait until the will has been read to see if the deceased expressed any opinions on the matter. Most organs have to be removed from a person who, though technically dead, is still on life support. You may wish you could go home and think it over for a few days but you don't have time.

## T Know Who Can Be a Donor

The short answer is that anyone in good health under the age of seventy-five who dies in hospital is a potential donor. In reality, it is not as simple as that.

### Must the person die in hospital?

Generally yes, although there is one exception to this. The reason is that the body must not be allowed to deteriorate before the organs can be removed. Exactly what this means and how this is prevented is explained below.

### What criteria must the deceased meet?

Because of the need for organs to be in good condition when they are removed, the donor needs to be:

- Clinically dead.

- On life support to allow the body's main functions – though not those of the brain – to be maintained.

- In good general health with no illnesses or diseases which might affect the organs or be transmitted to the recipient. Moreover, the deceased's relatives must give permission for the transplant operation to go ahead.

When someone dies, the body – but not the brain – can be kept functioning by a life-support machine. This does not mean that the person can be brought back to life: he is dead, and without life support the body's functions will cease entirely.

The phrase 'clinically dead' is a way of describing this situation. The person is dead in every meaning of the term but the body is prevented from deteriorating, as it otherwise would, by a machine taking over some of the functions of the brain, such as pumping blood around the body, and ensuring oxygen reaches the lungs and blood supply.

Another phrase often used to describe such a person is 'brainstem dead'. This is because tests on brainstem activity are used to determine whether death has actually occurred, or whether the person is simply in a deep coma.

The brainstem is the part of the brain which controls the human body's most essential tasks – breathing, heart-beat and conscious-ness. As long as someone's body can perform these tasks, doctors know that the brainstem is still functioning and that person is alive, even if he is deeply unconscious. However, if the body cannot perform the tasks unaided – without life support – he may have suffered brainstem death. If after tests have been carried out this diagnosis is confirmed, the person is officially declared dead.

It is often very hard for relatives to accept the idea of brainstem death. After all, someone is dead or he is not. Is brainstem death something different? As explained above, brainstem death is not something different but is a way of measuring death.

If you have been told that your relative is brainstem dead, you will probably want to see him to say goodbye. Do not be surprised if he does not look dead at all. That is because he will be on life support.

When transplant surgery first began, one of the fears voiced was that organs might be taken from a patient who was still alive, perhaps because doctors had wrongly diagnosed death or because of their keenness to use organs from someone who was clearly going to die at some stage in the near future. These fears were unfounded, but nevertheless they existed.

Since then, very strict guidelines have been laid down about how doctors are to confirm brainstem death, and these might help reassure you if you still have any lingering doubts as to whether your loved one is alive or dead. In brief, the procedure is:

- A series of specific tests must be carried out on the patient.

- These tests must be carried out twice, with an interval of several hours in between.

- The doctors carrying out the tests must be very senior doctors.

- The doctor carrying out the first set of tests must be completely independent of the one carrying out the second set.

There are five simple tests which are performed on the patient. None of these is intrusive or undignified, or will harm the patient in any way if he is still alive.

Only if both sets of tests show there is no sign that the brainstem is working at all is the patient declared dead.

If a person is brainstem dead but on life support and his relatives agree to organ removal, that person is known as a 'beating-heart' donor.

## ➊ Understand the Procedure

If you are called to a hospital and told your relative is very near death, you may be asked if you will give your permission for organ donation. The person who asks you will be a doctor, a senior nurse or the transplant co-ordinator for the hospital. This means, first, that they will have had experience in making this request and therefore will do so in a way which causes you the minimum of distress, and second, that they are in a position to answer any questions you may have.

They will tell you that the first set of tests for brainstem death have been carried out, if the person is already on life support and appears to have died, or say that these tests will be carried out as soon as the death occurs.

If you have agreed to a transplant, or are actively considering it, some hours must now elapse before the tests are repeated. During this time you will be allowed to sit by the bedside and say your goodbyes if you wish.

While this is happening, the transplant co-ordinator will contact the United Kingdom Transplant Support Services (UKTSS) and warn them that there might be a possible donor. Everyone involved will be aware that you might, and have the right to, decide against transplant and you will not be pressured to do so.

The second set of tests will then be carried out. If they show that brainstem death has indeed occurred, you may be offered the opportunity to see the life-support machine disconnected for a short time so you can verify that the person's body is indeed unable to function on its own any more. This is the point at which the person is officially declared dead.

If you then give your permission for transplant to go ahead, the body will be taken to theatre for the organs to be removed. You might decide to remain in the hospital to be with the deceased when he returns from theatre or you might decide to go home. Do not be put off seeing the deceased because you fear he will have been disfigured in some way by the operation: all wounds will have been sewn up in the normal way.

You can then start the process of registering the death and arranging for a funeral director in the normal way.

## How a recipient is found

While the last brainstem tests are being performed, the transplant co-ordinator will have set in motion a well-established procedure which enables a hospital with donor organs to find out who is in need of those organs, and where in the country they are.

What happens is that the hospital will phone the transplant co-ordinator for that region telling them that a donor might be available. The transplant co-ordinator then phones the UKTSS, which co-ordinates activities nationwide and in Ireland. In this way, everyone involved can find out very quickly indeed which patients are in urgent need, what their requirements are and where they live. Thus, a small boy dying of liver failure in, for example, Sheffield might be given a chance to live by the death of someone in London.

## ❶ Know What Organs Can Be Successfully Transplanted

### Kidneys

The success rate from kidney transplants in this country is now extremely high – a marvellous seventy per cent of recipients gain another five years or more of life. Unfortunately, there are still many people waiting for donated organs, and until they receive them they must remain on dialysis.

Kidneys can be taken from a wide age range of people – from a child as young as two to an elderly person up to seventy years of age, provided that person was healthy. The normal procedure is to take the kidneys from a person who has been on life support, but this is one of the times where they can be taken from someone who is dead on arrival at hospital, provided this occurs within an hour of death.

## Corneas

The cornea is the front part of the eye, and damage or disease to this area is a common cause of blindness. Transplantation is highly successful.

This is one time when the deceased does not have to have died in hospital to make donation possible: the requirement is that the corneas are removed within twelve hours of death. This is ample time, if the relatives and doctor act swiftly, for the deceased to be ferried to hospital by ambulance and the operation to take place.

There is no age requirement, so elderly people who wish to offer organs for transplantation can have their wish to help others accepted, as least as far as the gift of sight is concerned.

## Liver

The liver is the organ which acts to cleanse the blood, among other functions. Liver transplantation is relatively new, but even so the short-term survival rates are good.

The donor must have been classified as brainstem dead in hospital, so that life support could be continued until the liver could be removed. Livers are not taken from patients already dead before they reach life support facilities.

The upper age limit for donation is usually fifty-five years of age. There is no lower limit.

## Heart and Lung

This operation carries an eighty per cent survival rate for the first year, and some patients who have had the operation have lived for far longer.

There is no specific upper age limit for donation, but the donor must be young and healthy.

## ❶ Can You Offer the Organs of a Child For Transplantation?

Yes, and they are needed. Everyone will have seen urgent heart-rending appeals on television for donors for small children. The good news is that, where donors are available, children tend to do extremely well after the operation. The bad news is that there are not enough donors. Many people who would gladly have offered another child the chance of life after the tragic death of their own simply are not prepared for the decision because they have not had the chance to think beforehand whether this is something they would want.

## ❶ Know the Procedure if the Deceased Has Donated His Body for Medical Education

This is something the deceased must have arranged during his lifetime. If you have just read the will and discovered that the deceased wanted his body left for medical education (use by medical students), there is nothing you can do about it unless the deceased filled in the correct forms while he was alive.

If the deceased did fill in these forms, he should have put them somewhere safe and easy to find. If you find these forms you need to contact the specific medical school and tell them about the death. They will then arrange with a funeral director (they will organize everything) for the body to be collected. There is nothing you need do.

Be aware that even if the deceased has made all the correct arrangements, the offer of his body might still be declined if:

- He died as a result of certain illnesses.

- The coroner has become involved.

- The death took place somewhere which makes it impractical for the medical school to arrange collection.

The body can still be buried or cremated in the normal way when it is released by the medical school, which will bear the costs of a simple funeral. They will also make all the arrangements, if required – indeed, some insist on this and on the place of burial. Many others will release the body to the care of the bereaved and a funeral can be arranged in the normal way. In this case, though, the cost of the funeral will be yours.

# 23

# Caring for the Deceased's Pet

An enormous number of people in this country keep a pet – mostly cats and dogs, but also budgerigars, canaries, ferrets, pigeons and even snakes. When these are family pets there is usually no problem: if one member of the family dies as the pet stays in its home and is cared for by the remaining members of that family. The real problem occurs where the deceased is a single person, perhaps elderly, when the pet was a much-loved companion. After the death, particularly if it was unexpected, the pet remains at home, possibly unfed and certainly grieving until someone comes to take care of it. What happens to the pet if the deceased left no close relatives, or those relatives are unable to take it in? Who can you turn to for help? And what do you do while you are trying to make arrangements for the pet? This can be quite daunting, especially if you are not yourself an animal lover. Don't panic! There is help at hand, if you know where to look for it.

## ❶ Find Out Exactly What the Situation Is

You must find out as soon as possible if the deceased kept a pet and if so, where it is and who (if anybody) is taking care of it.

### Where the death was unexpected

If the death occurred at home and you are present at the death you will at least know that a pet exists and what it is. Even so, in the shock of the moment it is easy to overlook a cat slinking around the back of the sofa or the unfed budgie in the cage downstairs. Even worse, the pet might be locked out, waiting in vain to come in for its meal. Check out the situation and take a few seconds to see that the pet is at least fed and has something to drink. You can think about longer-term care later.

If the death occurs at hospital, especially if this is not the deceased's local hospital – perhaps he was visiting you – the problem is slightly greater, but so is the need to determine the situation. It is even worse if you don't know or have to hand the addresses of the deceased's friends and neighbours. It is hard to have to focus on what may seem like a small and troublesome problem at this time, but remember that most people who keep pets are extremely attached to them and the deceased would undoubtedly have wanted to ensure the pet is not left abandoned. There are steps you can take, even from a distance, to find out what the situation is:

- Ask the nurses who tended the deceased during his stay in hospital if he was conscious at any stage, and if so, whether he talked about a pet and whether it is being looked after by anyone at the moment. Elderly people in particular will often worry about an untended animal and if the deceased was able to talk he will often have shared these worries with nurses.

- Phone anyone who might have known the deceased and ask whether he kept a pet. You also need to know what it is. A cat or dog might create mess if left unattended for two or three hours and whereas that is certainly undesirable, the animal will not die in that time. Other pets may be more fragile.

- Find out exactly how long the deceased has been away from home. Perhaps he was only in hospital for a few hours before the death occurred, or perhaps it has been a day or more. This tells you how urgent the problem is.

- If you don't have the keys to the deceased's home, explain the situation to the hospital staff. They will have put the deceased's possessions away safely – at night they will have locked them away – and provided you can prove you are close to the deceased they may give you the keys so that you, or someone else you trust, can gain access to the home.

- If the deceased had been visiting you, try to remember what he said about care of the pet: possibly he had arranged for a neighbour to feed it. In that case, the problem is less urgent. You should, however, contact the neighbour if you can and tell him what has occurred.

Remember, if the death was unexpected the pet is unlikely to have been left alone for a long period. You must, however, make every effort to find out what has happened.

## Where the death was expected

In this case, it is quite possible that someone is looking after the pet, especially if the deceased is in hospital and had time to make arrangements.

## 🅣 If There is a Pet, Take Emergency Action to Make Sure It Has Food, Water and Shelter

If several hours have passed and you are still not sure whether there is a pet, or you know one exists but not whether it is being fed and looked after, you must take more positive steps. If you are not an animal lover – and not everyone is – this might seem like a confounded nuisance, but the pet is now helpless and totally dependent on someone coming to its aid.

Unless you have managed to find someone who lives close to the deceased's home and has a key, you can:

- Go yourself to check the situation.

- Send someone you trust.

- Phone the RSPCA.

This is now a priority.

### Go yourself to check the situation

Hopefully, you will not be too far away from the deceased's home. If you do decide to go yourself, use the journey constructively. If you are driving, think about the things you have to do in the next few days and prioritize them. If you are travelling by train or bus, make a list of what you need to do next and who you must contact.

### Send someone you trust

The alternative is to find a 'volunteer' prepared to go. If you can't contact any of the deceased's other relatives or friends, ask your own friends or family. It is highly likely that one of them will take on the task, if only to help you out. It must, obviously, be someone you trust absolutely as he will be going into the deceased's unoccupied home.

If you are sending someone else, particularly if it is one of your friends, it is sensible to give him a letter with your name, address and phone number on it detailing the situation, just in case the police or a neighbour suspect him of burglary. Make sure you will be in phone contact at the time he is physically in the house. If the friend is particularly nervous about going into a stranger's house he could always pop into the local police station first and explain what is going on. The police can check with you and with the hospital if necessary.

## Phone the RSPCA

It might be that, for one reason or another, none of these options are open to you. Perhaps you yourself are elderly or disabled, or you live a long way away. In that case, you should phone the RSPCA.

The Royal Society for the Prevention of Cruelty to Animals is always prepared to help where an animal needs aid, and you will find their phone number in Appendix 5. At the very least they can advise you how long it is safe to leave the pet before it suffers real hardship. In an emergency you can ask them to intervene. The problems are to enable them to gain access to the house, and to prove that the deceased is dead.

The second problem is easier to tackle. You can ask someone at the hospital to phone the RSPCA, or you can ask the hospital to phone the police to confirm the death, then ask the police to contact them.

Enabling them to gain access is more tricky. You cannot sanction them to break in as this means the house will then have a broken window or front door. The best thing to do is to courier the keys to them (without the address attached in case they are lost). Arguably, this is an urgent and essential expense you can claim back from the estate.

By far the best solution, though, is to go yourself if at all possible.

## ❶ Approach the Pet Carefully

Let us assume that you yourself have opted to go and make sure the pet has food and water. Not everyone is an animal lover, and not every animal lover is at ease with every type of pet. How do you make sure you are not going to be attacked, bitten or scratched?

It depends, of course, on the identity of the pet. The first thing to remember, though, is that, whatever the animal is, by now it will be hungry and thirsty and will probably be extremely pleased to see a human being.

### Dogs

If you are really afraid of dogs, phone the RSPCA and ask someone to come with you. If you think you can handle the situation on your own, remember a few simple guidelines and there should be no problems.

- Don't be afraid if it barks: most dogs will if someone comes to the door. This doesn't mean the dog is hostile – it simply means it is behaving like a dog.

- Speak to it in a firm, quiet voice. If you convey that you are not hostile or afraid, it is likely to respond in kind.

- When you open the door, hold your ground unless it is clearly hostile. It may jump up a few times but, especially if it has been alone for a while, this may be through pleasure.

- Let it sniff you if it wants. Don't make any sudden moves while it is doing so.

- See if it is wagging its tail: this is not an infallible indicator of pleasure, but it is often a good sign.

- Offer it a handful of dog biscuits.

- Don't show any fear: a dog will pick this up immediately. If you are afraid, take a slow deep breath and relax your shoulders: you will feel better at once.

- Look at the dog, but don't stare at it.

- Watch out for danger signs: if the dog stiffens, snarls, holds its tail high or bares its teeth at you, DO stand still, DO back away very slowly, DON'T run – it will chase you.

You might also get a warmer reception if you open a tin of food before you enter, and spoon some on to a saucer: a hungry animal will find this a much more attractive meal than your ankles. Stay calm, speak quietly. Don't run. The most useful precaution you can take is to wear a long coat and a pair of thick gloves – leather gloves are fine, gardening gloves are even better.

If it has messed on the carpet, look for or buy some rubber gloves and find some newspaper or a cloth to clear up the faeces or urine. Don't be angry with the dog – if it was locked in, it had no choice. Be sure to wash your hands afterwards.

## Cats

The worst things a cat can do to you are either scratch you (hardly a terminal injury) or shoot through the door and disappear the moment you open it.

The first problem is easily solved. Wear a long coat or trousers and gloves. Cats can rarely jump high enough to scratch you anywhere else.

The second is more difficult. You have made a special effort to come here and the animal has fled. What do you do?

Try the food-on-a saucer trick. Don't attempt to catch the cat, even if it is lurking nearby. It will already be upset and edgy and will probably leap up the nearest tree, or run even further away if you scare it. Leave the door open, put the saucer down just in front of it then stand back to see what happens. It may take a few minutes but the cat should get the message.

If it doesn't respond – and some cats simply hate strangers and will not come near them no matter what – wait as long as you can and then you have two options, depending on what the situation is.

- If you know the deceased was on good terms with his neighbours, although you perhaps don't know their names and couldn't contact them beforehand, you could see them, explain the situation and ask them to put out food for the next few days while you work out a longer term solution. Most neighbours will be only too happy to oblige.

- If this is not possible – perhaps the deceased was on bad terms with his neighbours or it is a rough area and you think it a bad idea to approach them – then ring the RSPCA. They will come round and try to catch the cat. Even if you cannot stay, once you have described it they can keep an eye out for it: cats are highly territorial and it will return home sooner or later.

The other thing to do is to clean its litter tray, if it has one. Cats are scrupulously clean and really hate using dirty litter. If the tray has already been used a few times they would far prefer to use the nice clean carpet.

Assuming the cat has not run away and is safely indoors, if it is accustomed to going out, and you are not going to be around for the rest of that day, use your discretion. It really is better not to lock it out: you cannot guarantee when you will be back or what the weather will be in the meantime. Go to the pet shop and invest in some cat litter and a tray – it will only cost you a couple of pounds. When you have put the litter into the tray, show it to the cat and lift him gently on to it. Especially if he has just eaten the food you've provided, he'll soon get the idea.

## Birds

You should have no problems here. Even if it is a bird with a large beak such as a parrot, leather gloves and an arm's-length approach should enable you to avoid injury. Look around the house for a packet of its food and make sure it has some in the cage. You also need to make sure it has some water.

The bigger problem is cleaning its cage: for some birds, a dirty cage can be dangerous. If you really can't face the task or are not sure what to do, phone the RSPCA.

## Hamsters

Most hamsters are tame and friendly (the odd one will bite, but it's not going to do much damage). Their immediate needs are for food and water. Hamsters eat a variety things, including fresh greens, but in an emergency you can use packets of hamster food. Make sure it has some water. It will only dirty one area of the cage so this can easily be swept out. Above all, make sure it doesn't escape because you might find it difficult to catch it again.

## Pigeons/ferrets/snakes/exotic animals

Phone the RSPCA. Don't try to deal with the situation. The pet(s) may well not be dangerous – pigeons don't exactly have a reputation for being hostile to humans – but constant, expert care is necessary and this is not your main aim at this moment. Never, never think of trying to feed a snake!

## ● Know What to Feed the Pet

If it is very hungry it should eat almost anything suitable for that type of pet. A quick raid on a local supermarket should reveal a variety of tins of cat, dog and bird food. It is a good idea to buy a couple of tins, choosing different varieties – the pet may have a strong aversion to one. Cats, especially, can be very fussy eaters.

Always leave it water to drink. Don't leave milk for cats – it is a myth that all cats like milk and it is positively harmful to some, even though they might like the taste. You cannot go wrong with water.

## ● Arrange Medium-Term Care

The pet will need daily care – feeding, cleaning and company. Hopefully, you or someone in your family can do this. It is a very good task for children, if they are old enough, and will help them feel they are doing something for the deceased. If you or your family cannot do this, see if the neighbours might help, but be sure that they are honest before you hand over any keys. Failing that, as always, phone the RSPCA or a similar organization.

If you can find the animal's vaccination certificates, think about approaching a local cattery (some accept dogs and other animals as well). If they can't take the animal, or you can't find the vaccination certificate, ask them if they know of a local organization which might help.

## ❶ Arrange a Permanent Home for the Pet

This is something you are going to have to do sooner or later. Unless you are absolutely sure you want the pet and can care for it, it is better to arrange short-term care in the deceased's house while you work out what to do, otherwise the pet will have two bewildering changes of home in a very short space of time. Don't forget, it has already lost its owner.

Don't give the pet to the first person who offers, or to a stranger, unless you are absolutely sure that this person will give it a good and stable home.

## ❶ Decide Whether to Have it Put Down

This is something you might want to consider if the pet is elderly, ill or pining. Otherwise, try to home it. If you do have to have it put down and it was deeply loved, you should know that you can bury pets in special pet cemeteries. Perhaps you could consider this as a last act for the deceased, even if you yourself are dubious about its value. The RSPCA has a list of pet cemeteries.

## ❶ Check Whether the Deceased Has Already Thought About This Problem

At least one organization runs a scheme which allows people to decide in advance what will happen to their pet after their death. This is the Emergency Pet Alert Scheme run by the Wood Green Animal Shelter in London. Despite the Shelter being based in London, the scheme operates nationwide.

Consider whether the deceased might have joined this scheme, (which is free for those over sixty if they cannot pay the £5 minimum fee, thus making it attractive to them). If so, he would have had his details, those of the pet, and those of the person who should be contacted in an emergency recorded on a computer, which can be contacted via a twenty-four hour hotline. He would have been given a small card to carry on him – rather like a donor card – and a larger card which stays in the house. Search the house for this card, and ask whether the smaller card has been found among the deceased's personal possessions. If so, phone the hotline and they will arrange to collect the pet and take it to its new home. (Where the deceased knows the relatives would be unwilling to take the pet, he might have asked for it to be homed in one of their sanctuaries.) If the deceased joined this scheme, it will save you a lot of problems.

## ❶ Know Your Organizations

In an emergency, phone an animal care organization. It doesn't matter how small or stupid you think your query is, they would rather hear from you than let a pet suffer.

The RSPCA will always accept calls and help if at all possible. Phone directory enquiries for a local number if you don't know it. If necessary, they can advise on specialist animal aid groups (hedgehogs, ferrets etc). They will take the pet if you cannot cope but will not guarantee to rehouse it. Some may, unfortunately, have to be put to sleep. (see Appendix 5 for the number of their headquarters.)

Another worthwhile organization is the PDSA – People's Dispensary for Sick Animals (branches throughout the country). They can offer you advice and talk to you about rehoming. (Their main number is given in Appendix 5.)

It is worth looking through a copy of the local paper, as there are many (too many to list) small charities run by local people with the aim of helping animals.

The Wood Green Animal Shelter in London runs the Emergency Pet Aid Scheme. If the deceased was a member, they will travel anywhere in the country to collect the pet. They have a policy of not destroying animals they cannot rehome, but sending them to one of their sanctuaries. Their phone number is given in Appendix 5. (It might be worth thinking about this scheme for yourself, if you have a pet.)

# Appendices

Appendices

# 1

# Notices for the Press

You can, of course, use any variation of these you wish. Be warned, however, that some papers will not accept notices for the Deaths column which are too unusual. For these sample notices, a fictitious family named Smith has been used. You, of course, will insert the names of the deceased and his relatives as appropriate and change husband to wife etc where appropriate.

First sentences

John George Smith – very peacefully on [date].

Smith, John, on [date], after a long illness bravely borne.

Smith, John, at home in Salisbury on [date], after a long and courageous fight against illness.

On [date], peacefully at home [at Far View Nursing Home], John Smith, late of New Town, Salisbury.

On [date], suddenly, John Smith, aged 50 years.

On [date] as the result of a car accident, John Smith, deeply loved husband of Martha.

Family descriptions

Most death notices contain some description of the family. Typically, this will go after the deceased's name and date of death, either in the same sentence or in a new one.

...beloved husband of Martha, loving father of Fred and grandfather to Eileen.

...much loved husband of Martha.

...loving and deeply loved husband of Martha.

...dearly loved father, grandfather and great-grandfather.

...devoted husband and father.

## Funeral details

The funeral will be held at [place and date].

Funeral service at [place and date] followed by cremation at the New Crematorium.

Private family funeral. (In this case, this is all you would say: you would not give the place and date of the funeral in the notice as anyone who is invited will be contacted privately).

Prayers at 8.00pm, 18 New Street, New Town. (You might use a notice like this when you are holding a private family funeral and don't want to put the details in the notice, when you know the deceased had friends who might be uneasy about attending that particular place of worship, or when you have simply decided not to hold any religious ceremony at the church or crematorium.)

Enquiries to [name of funeral director]. (You might use this when you do not want people seeing the notice to phone or write directly to you for details of the death, how to get to the church or crematorium etc).

## Donations and flowers

Donations, if desired, to [name and address of organization].

At his wish no flowers please, but donations to...

Family flowers only but donations please to...

Donations to a charity of your choice.

Donations invited to...

No flowers please. Donations instead to...

Note: If there is no statement about donations, most people will assume that flowers are to be sent.

## Other sentences

These are not essential, but some people like to include a phrase which sums up their feelings:

Gone but not forgotten.

At last at peace.

Note: The phrases given in Appendix 3 can be used here instead of these examples.

A memorial service will be held at [place and date].(You might use this when you want the actual funeral to be private, but you want the deceased's friends to have the chance to participate in a service.)

Former volunteer worker for [*name of organization*].(You can use this sentence to describe a job or volunteer post held.)

# 2

# Hymns and Texts

Some of these hymns are sung in Anglican churches, some in Catholic, some are universally popular and sung anywhere.

There are many different hymn books in use so specific page references are no help: instead, the first line is given. You can then look this up in whichever hymnbook is applicable.

You may find this list jogs your memory and you recognize hymns you, or perhaps the deceased, sang in the past.

- Abide with me
- Be still, and know I am with you
- Be still my soul
- Day is done
- Do not be afraid
- Going home, going home
- Guide me, O thou great Redeemer
- I'll be with you to the end of the world
- Jesus, remember me
- Lead, kindly light
- My love for you will never leave you
- The Lord is my shepherd
- Till the end of my days
- We are bound for the promised land
- We will walk through the valley
- When the day grows cold

## Readings and texts

### A modern psalm for those left behind

Relatives and friends, I am about to leave: my last breath does not say 'goodbye', for my love for you is truly timeless beyond the touch of death. I leave myself not to the undertaker, for decoration in his house of the dead, but to your memory, with love.

I leave my thoughts, my laughter, my dreams to you whom I have treasured beyond gold and precious gems. I give you what no thief can steal, the memories of our times together: the tender, love-filled moments, the successes we shared, the hard times that brought us closer together and the roads we have walked side by side.

I also leave you a solemn promise that after I am home in the bosom of God, I will still be present, whenever and wherever you call on me. My energy will be drawn to you by the magnet of our love. Whenever you are in need, call me – I will come to you, with my arms full of wisdom and light to open up your blocked paths, to untangle your knots and to be your avenue to God.

And all I take with me as I leave is your love and the millions of memories of all that we have shared. So I truly enter my new life as a millionaire. Fear not nor grieve at my departure, you whom I have loved so much, for my roots and yours are forever entwined.

### Traditional psalms

The Lord is my shepherd, I shall not want.
Fresh and green are the pastures
where he gives me repose.
Near restful waters he leads me,
to revive my drooping spirit.
(Note: there are many versions of this.)
Yea, though I walk in the valley of darkness
yet will I fear none ill.
For thou art with me,
and thy rod and staff comfort me still.

### Second letter of St Paul to the Corinthians

We know that when the tent that we live in on earth is folded up, there is a house built by God for us, an everlasting home not made by human hands, in the Heavens.

We are always full of confidence, then, when we remember that to live in the body means to be exiled from the Lord, going as we do by faith and not by sight: we are full of confidence, I say, and actually want to be exiled from the body and make our home with the Lord. Whether we are living in the body or exiled from it, we are intent on pleasing him. For all the truth about us will be brought out in the law court of Christ, and each of us will get what he deserves for the things he did in the body, good or bad.

## Gospel according to John

I am the resurrection and the life.
Whoever believes in me, even though he dies he will live,
and whoever dies and believes in me
will never die.

## From the book of Wisdom

The souls of the virtuous are in the hands of God.
no torment shall ever touch them.
In the eyes of the unwise, they did appear to die,
their going looked like a disaster,
their leaving us like annihilation;
but they are in peace.
If they experienced punishment as men see it,
their hope was rich with immortality;
slight was their affliction, great will their blessing be.
God has put them to the test
and proved them worthy to be with him;
he has tested them like gold in a furnace,
and accepted them as a holocaust.
They who trust in him will understand the truth,
those who are faithful will live with him in love,
for grace and mercy await those he has chosen.

## A reading from the book of Wisdom

The virtuous man, though he die before his time, will find rest.
Length of days is not what makes age honourable,
nor number of years the true measure of life:
understanding, this is man's grey hairs,
untarnished life, this is ripe old age.

He has sought to please God, so God has loved him;
as he was living among sinners, he has been taken up.
He has been carried off so that evil may not warp his understanding
or treachery seduce his soul:
for the fascination of evil throws good things into the shade,

and the whirlwind of desire corrupts a simple heart.
 Coming to perfection in so short a while, he achieved long life:
his soul was pleasing to the Lord,
he has taken him quickly from the wickedness around him.
Yet people look on uncomprehending:
it does not enter their heads
that grace and mercy await the chosen of the Lord;
and protection his holy ones.

# 3

# Sample Inscriptions

Change the 'he' to 'she' where appropriate, and vice versa. Don't forget that you may only be allowed a certain number of words, and you will also need to add the deceased's name, date of death and perhaps, date of birth.

A gentle man.

A godly man who served the Lord all his days.

Absent from the body
Present with the Lord.

All through your suffering great patience you bore
Till God called you home to suffer no more.

Always in our thoughts
Forever in our hearts.

As the bird free of its cage seeks the heights
So the Christian soul in death flies home to God.

At rest.

Forever in our thoughts.

Great love lives on.

He lived life to the fullest.

He touched the lives of many.

His courage, his smile, his grace, gladdened the hearts of those who have the privilege of loving him.

His life a beautiful memory
His absence a silent grief.

I am the resurrection and the life. He that believeth in Me, though he were dead, yet shall he live.

I go to prepare a place for you that where I am, there you may also be.

I have fought the good fight. I have finished my course. I have kept the faith.

I will dwell in the house of the Lord forever.

If our love could have saved him
He would not have died.

In ever loving memory of a dear husband and father [name] who fell asleep [*date*] aged [*years*].

In God's care [*or keeping*].

Love is eternal.

May God be with you and comfort you.

May she rest in peace with God.

Our brief partings on earth will appear one day as nothing beside the joy of eternity together.

Rest after weariness.

Rest, O weary traveller, for with the dawn comes great joy.

Reunited.

She filled every second of her life with laughter, love and happiness.

She is not far away.

She loved everyone.

The Lord is my shepherd.

Those we love remain with us for love itself lives on.

To live in the hearts of those we love is not to die.

Too dearly loved to be forgotten.

While he lives cherished in our memories, he is never far away.

While we have time, let us do good.

## Children
A tiny flower lent not given
To bud on earth and bloom in Heaven.

In Heaven one angel more.
Jesus called a little child unto him.
On earth one gentle soul the less.
Step softly, a dream lies buried here.

# 4

# Sample Letters

In all these letters an imaginary name and address is used. We are assuming that your name is Mildred Smith, that you live at 51 Egbert Street, New Town and that it is your uncle George who has died.

Before you write most of these letters you really need an official document which states that the death took place. You might also need a copy of your probate document, or of the will. Common sense will tell you that the people you are contacting need to be sure of the death, and that you are someone who has the right to handle these matters.

Some letters need to be phrased in different ways depending upon circumstances, and also depending on how close the recipient was to the deceased, so a choice of wording is suggested.

Important – take photocopies of any important letters you send out together with any enclosures. All reasonable costs can be claimed back from the estate.

# Friends and Relations

51 Egbert Street
New Town

30 April 19xx

Dear...

I'm afraid I have some bad news for you. Uncle George died
in hospital/at home last Thursday.

It came as a great shock to everyone as he was in excellent
health. What happened was that he...

[*Alternatively*] As you probably know, he had been ill for some
time so this wasn't entirely unexpected, but even so it was a great
shock to everyone when it finally happened.

The funeral will take place next Monday, 4 May. There will be
a service at St Faith, Carstairs Street, New Town at 11.00 am,
followed by the interment at Oscar Road Cemetery at noon.
I know it may not be convenient for you to come for family
reasons, but if you would like to attend, perhaps you could give
me a ring or write to me.

[*Alternatively*]. The date of the funeral has still to be arranged
but it should be some time next week. I know it may not be
convenient for you attend, but if you would like to, perhaps you
could give me a ring or write to me and I will send you further
details as soon as I know them.

[*Alternatively*] The family has decided the funeral is to be
a private one, but if you want to, please send flowers/make
a donation to [name of organization].

I am very sorry to have to break this news to you.

Yours sincerely,


Mildred Smith

**Ⓗ**  Unless you are absolutely certain that the friend or relative
will want to attend the funeral it is tactful to make some face-
saving comment suggesting that they might have valid reasons
for not being able to do so – even if you know these reasons
to be false!

# Accommodation

51 Egbert Street
New Town

30 April 19xx

[*Address*]

Dear Sir/Madam,

This is to notify you that my uncle, George Frederick Smith of 3 Green Close, New Town died on 25 April 19xx, and I enclose a copy of his Death Certificate for your records. I understand that you hold the mortgage on his house/flat.

Please advise me as to how you wish me to proceed in order to expedite matters.

Yours sincerely,

Mildred Smith

**H** Handling matters this way means you don't have to second-guess their procedures. They will write and tell you what they want.

## Accommodation

51 Egbert Street
New Town

30 April 19xx

[*Address*]

Dear Sir/Madam,

This is to notify you that my uncle, George Frederick Smith of 3 Green Close, New Town died on 25 April 19xx.

I understand the rent on that property is paid up to [*date*].

[*As executor of his estate*] it is my intention to clear his possessions and vacate the premises as soon as is practicable. I will notify you of the date upon which I will return the keys.

I will ensure that the appropriate utilities companies are notified and any bills paid out of his estate.

Yours faithfully,


Mildred Smith

🄗  Even though your uncle is dead, his estate is still protected by the law. If the tenancy runs until a specific date you cannot be forced to vacate the premises until that date. Don't let anyone try to convince you otherwise.

If the rent is paid and you vacate the premises before the end of the tenancy it is worth trying to negotiate a rent rebate.

If the rent is in arrears the estate must pay this money. Make it clear that at the earliest opportunity you will honour this commitment to save unpleasantness.

If the rent is in arrears and you have reason to believe the landlord is an unsavoury character, remove any valuables and mementoes from the property before you send this letter and negotiate payment of the debt afterwards. Some landlords ignore the legal process in favour of harassment and/or illegal seizure of property. Make sure, though, that you honour the debt if there is money in the estate or you will be putting yourself on the wrong side of the law.

# Benefits

51 Egbert Street
New Town

30 April 19xx

[Address]

Dear Sir/Madam,

I regret to inform you that my uncle, George Frederick Smith of 3 Green Close, New Town died on 25 April 19xx. [*I enclose a copy of the Death Certificate and the will.*]

I understand from his papers that he was in receipt of services/ benefits provided by you. [His claim/number was ........]. Could you please advise me as executor [*the executor, Mrs Anne Smith of 8 Acorn Terrace*] of any moneys owed to him. Please make all cheques payable to [*name of estate account*]. Could you also please advise of any moneys owed by his estate to you.

Yours sincerely,


Mildred Smith

**H**  You can use this letter for any government department.

It may be that the estate will continue to receive money owed to Uncle George. You need to specify the name of the account into which they should be paid as Uncle George's account will have been frozen. You cannot pay them into your account because that is in your name. You should send a copy of some document showing that you are the correct person with whom they must deal.

## Financial

51 Egbert Street
New Town

30 April 19xx

Financially Sound Insurance Co
[*Address*]

Dear Sir/Madam,

This is to notify you that my uncle, George Frederick Smith of 3 Green Close, New Town died on 25 April 19xx. As executor of his estate I enclose a copy of the Death Certificate [*will/grant of probate*] for your records. I understand that he has, or had, taken out life/house/contents insurance with your company. I regret that no further details are available at this stage. Please advise on your procedures in this situation.

[*Alternatively*] At the present time the will has not been read/located and no executor identified. I understand from his papers etc...

I will contact you as soon as more details are available.

Yours sincerely,

Mildred Smith

**H** As this involves money it is crucial that you put in writing to them the fact of the death and the date as soon as possible. You must send a copy of the Death Certificate at the very least. It is quite acceptable to say that at this stage you have no further details. Do this if you have only a suspicion that the deceased had dealings with them: they will soon tell you if he did not, and it means they are taking a task off your hands.

At some stage they will need a copy of the will and/or grant of probate. In this way they will know who the legal executor is and who they must deal with.

# Financial

51 Egbert Street
New Town

30 April 19xx

Private Medical Insurance Co
[*Address*]

Dear Sir/Madam,

This is to notify you that my uncle, George Frederick Smith of 3 Green Close, New Town died on 25 April 19xx. As executor of his estate I enclose a copy of the Death Certificate [*the will/grant of probate*] for your records. I understand from his papers that he has taken out medical insurance with your company. The details are as follows:

[*details*]

Please send the relevant forms to enable me [*the executor*] to make a claim on this insurance relating to his final illness/treatment.

[*Alternatively*] At the present time the will has not been read/located and no executor identified. I understand from his papers etc...

Yours sincerely,

Mildred Smith

**ⓗ**   Make doubly sure you keep photocopies of all correspondence relating to medical insurance. Firstly, a claim may already have been made in relation to treatment about which you know nothing, and secondly, you may have to forward papers to the medical authorities for signature, depending on the circumstances. It is very easy to lose track of exactly what is going on.

# Financial

51 Egbert Street
New Town

30 April 19xx

The Manager
High Street Branch
[*Bank/Building Society*]
[*Address*]

Dear Sir/Madam,

I regret to inform you that my uncle, George Frederick Smith of 3 Green Close, New Town, died on 25 April 19xx. I enclose a copy of the Death Certificate [*and the will*].

I understand from his papers that he was a customer of your bank. His account details are:

[*details*]

Could you please freeze his account pending instructions as to the disposition of money contained therein, and also advise me [*the executor*] of any other accounts or assets which you may hold on his behalf.

Yours faithfully,


Mildred Smith


**H**   One account number is sufficient. The bank/building society will be able to use this to locate any other accounts or assets, such as stocks and shares.

Banks and building societies are usually very helpful under such circumstances. If you are unfortunate enough to meet difficulties remember that your uncle paid for their services. Demand the name of the Area Manager – the bank must give it to you – and send a copy of this letter to him, together with an explanation of why you are taking this action.

# Financial

51 Egbert Street
New Town

30 April 19xx

Flexible Friend Credit Card Co
[*Address*]

Dear Sir/Madam,

I regret to inform you that my uncle, George Frederick Smith of 3 Green Close, New Town, died on 25 April 19xx. I enclose a copy of the Death Certificate [*and the will*].

I understand from his papers that he was the holder of one of your credit cards. His account number is

[*details*]

Please send me [*the executor*] a statement of the amount owed to you. This debt will be settled immediately moneys from the estate become available.

Yours faithfully,


Mildred Smith

**ℍ**    It is crucial that you notify them as soon as possible in case of fraud. It may be that you have found old statements – thus knowing the account number – but not the card, which has fallen into criminal hands.

Check that Uncle George hadn't taken out a policy which cancelled the debt on his death.

# Medical

51 Egbert Street
New Town

30 April 19xx

Dr...
Arthritis Clinic
General Hospital
[*Address*]

Dear Dr......

I understand that my uncle, George Frederick Smith of 3 Green Close, New Town was a patient of yours. I regret to inform you that he died on 25 April 19xx.

I would like to thank you on behalf of the family for the care you have given him.

Please advise me if my uncle was in possession of any hospital property relating to his treatment by this department which I will, of course, return to you immediately.

Yours sincerely,


Mildred Smith

🅗    Even if the death took place in the hospital do not assume that individual clinics will have been notified. Hospital bureaucracy does not always work that way.

The rule of thumb is 'Would the deceased want me to make this letter more personal?', for example he might have had reason to be grateful to a particular nurse or doctor. If you have their name it would be nice to include it.

## Medical

New Town
30 April 19xx

Mr...
Chiropodist
[*Address*]

Dear Mr...

I understand that my uncle, George Frederick Smith of 3 Green Close, New Town was a patient of yours and I regret to inform you that he died on 25 April 19xx.

I would like to thank you on behalf of the family for the care you have given him.

Please advise me as executor of his estate of any unpaid bills, which should be sent to me at the above address.

[*Alternatively*] Please advise the executor, Mrs Ann Green, of my uncle's estate of any unpaid bills. Her address is [*address*].

Yours sincerely,

Mildred Smith

**H**   It is not necessary to send a copy of the Death Certificate under normal circumstances.

It is wise to have all bills sent directly to the executor if this is not you, as he is responsible for paying them.

## Medical

51 Egbert Street
New Town

30 April 19xx

Records Office
[*Address*]

Dear Sir/Madam,

I regret to inform you that my uncle, George Frederick Smith of 3 Green Close, New Town died on 25 April 19xx and I therefore enclose his medical card [*blood donor's appointment card*].

Yours sincerely,


Mildred Smith


**ⓗ**  It sounds terse but is there really any need to say more? The letter is likely to be dealt with by a clerk who did not know your uncle personally. Your address is on the letter if they should need to contact you.

The address to which you should address the letter should be on the card.

This letter can also be used, suitably amended, for the return of a passport (see 'State' on page 104).

## Organizations/Clubs

51 Egbert Street
New Town

30 April 19xx

[*Address*]

Dear Sir/Madam,

I regret to inform you of the death of my uncle, George
Frederick Smith of 3 Green Close, New Town, on 25 April 19xx.

I understand from his papers that he was a member of your
organization/club.

Would you please advise me as to whether your
club/organization has a policy of refunding the unexpired portion
of the membership.

Yours sincerely,


Mildred Smith

**(H)**   If at all possible, this letter should be personalized. If it was a
political or charitable organization you could make some
comment about how he very much supported the aims of the
organization. If it was a social or health club you could talk
about the benefits he received. It really doesn't matter whether
you know this to be the truth or not – if Uncle George made
the effort to pay a subscription he obviously approved of the
aims and gained some pleasure from membership. Writing
one extra sentence will take you only seconds.

## Utilities

51 Egbert Street
New Town

30 April 19xx

[*Telephone/Gas/Electricity Co*]
[*Address*]

Dear Sir/Madam,

A/C No:....

This is to inform you that my uncle, George Frederick Smith of 3, Green Close, New Town died on 25 April 19xx.

Please would you forward all bills for my attention to the above address [*to the executor of the estate, Mrs Anne Smith of 8, Acorn Terrace*], and they will receive prompt attention.

[*The premises will be vacated on 1 May 199x. I would be grateful if you would terminate the supply/service from that date and send the final account to the address detailed above.*]

Yours sincerely,


Mildred Smith


**H**   When you are writing to the electricity company it might be worth checking whether Uncle George had fridge or freezer insurance.

# 5

# Useful Addresses

**Age Concern England**
Astral House
1268 London Road
Norbury
London SW16 4ER

0181 679 8000

**Alder Centre**
**Royal Liverpool**
**Children's Hospital**
Alder Hey
Eaton Road
Liverpool L12 2AP

0151 228 4811

**W & F C Bonhams Auctioneers**
Montpelier Galleries
Montpelier Street
London SW7 1HH

0171 584 9161

**British Humanist Association**
Bradlaugh House
47 Theobald's Road
London WC1X 4SP

0171 430 0908

**British Organ Donors Society**
Balsham
Cambridge CB1 6DL

01223 893636

**Christies (Auction House)**
**South Kensington Ltd**
85 Old Brompton Road
London SW7 3JS

0171 581 7611

**The Compassionate Friends**
6 Denmark Street
Bristol BS1 5DQ

0117 9539639

**Cremation Society**
Brecon House
16-16a Albion Place
Maidstone
Kent ME14 5DZ

01622 688292/3

**Cruse**
Cruse House
126 Sheen Road
Richmond
Surrey TW9 1UR

0181 940 4818
*Helpline*: 0181 332 7227
9.30–5pm Mon–Fri

**DVLC**
Swansea SA99 1AR

Foundation for the Study of
Infant Deaths
35 Belgrave Square
London SW1X 8QB

0171 235 0965
*Helpline*: 0171 235 1721

HM Inspector of Anatomy
Department of Health
Wellington House
133–155 Waterloo Road
London SE1 8UG

0171 972 2000

*Law Society Gazette*
50–52 Chancery Lane
London WC2AA 1SX

0171 242 1222

*London Gazette*
PO Box 7923
London SE1 5ZH

0171 394 4580

National Association of
Funeral Directors
618 Warwick Road
Solihull
West Midlands  B91 1AA

0121 711 1343

National Association of
Memorial Masons
Crown Buildings
High Street
Aylesbury
Bucks HP20 1SL

01296 434750

National Association of Widows
54-7 Allison Street
Digbeth
Birmingham  B5 5TH

0121 643 8348

National Secular Society
Bradlaugh House
47 Theobald's Road
London WC1X 4SP

0171 430 0908

Natural Death Centre
20 Heber Road
London NW2 6AA

0181 208 2853

People's Dispensary for
Sick Animals (PDSA)
Head Office
Whitechapel Way
Priorslee
Telford
Salop TF2 9EA

01952 290999

Probate Personal
Applications Department
Principal Registry
of the Family Division
2nd Floor
Somerset House
Strand
London W2R 1LP

0171 936 6983

Public Record Office
Ruskin Avenue
Richmond
Surrey TW9 4DU

0181 876 3444

**RSPCA**
London Regional Office
PO Box 756
London SE25 5SF

0345 888999

**Sotheby's Auctioneers**
34 New Bond Street
London W1A 2AA

0171 493 8080

**War Pensions Directorate**
*Helpline*: 01253 858858

**Wood Green Animal Shelters**
601 Lordship Lane
Wood Green
London N22 5JG

0181 888 2351